Jaffna Tamil Grammar
The Essential Guide for Beginners

உ. நி. சப்தஸ்வரஜா

U. N. Sabthaswaraja

Tamil Language Centre

Jaffna Tamil Grammar
The Essential Guide for Beginners

U. N. Sabthaswaraja
Tamil Language Centre
First Edition January 2025

All proceeds from this book will go towards promoting Tamil language and culture.

For more information, email:
tamillanguagecentre@gmail.com

Contents

Introduction to Jaffna Tamil Grammar

Introduction to Jaffna Tamil Grammar

This book is crafted especially for adults seeking to learn spoken Jaffna Tamil as a second language, with a focus on practicality and real-life usage rather than traditional literary norms. The roots of this endeavor are deeply personal, intertwined with love and reverence for my grandparents, whose passion for the Tamil language inspired me to share its beauty with others.

I penned the first draft of this guide in 2019, but life's myriad responsibilities delayed its completion—until now. As I reflect on the past decade, this year marks the 10th anniversary of my grandparents' passing, a poignant reminder of the values they instilled in me. Their unwavering commitment to our language and culture ignited a fire in my heart; their legacy is the driving force behind my mission to teach Tamil.

Since 2004, I have dedicated my weekends to teaching Tamil in traditional Tamil schools. However, the traditional approach, primarily revolves around literary Tamil. Following my grandparents' passing in 2015, I recognised the urgent need for a paradigm shift in my method of teaching Tamil. I sought to create a resource that resonates more authentically with learners, bridging the gap between written and spoken Tamil.

To reach a broader audience, I launched 'The Tamil Channel' on YouTube in 2016, where I began producing short vocabulary and grammar videos. The positive response was overwhelming, and requests for online Tamil lessons surged. This prompted me to focus entirely on teaching spoken Tamil. Over the past five years, I have developed a targeted syllabus that addresses the needs of second-language learners, reflecting both the nuances of spoken Jaffna Tamil and the unique challenges faced by learners in the diaspora.

This book is more than just a grammar guide; it is a heartfelt tribute to my grandparents and a testament to the passion they fostered in me. It is designed to empower you with the skills and confidence to communicate effectively in Jaffna Tamil, enriching your connection to our language and culture. Together, let us embark on this journey, as we delve into the rich dynamic realm of spoken Tamil in all its true and authentic beauty.

How to Use This Book

This book is designed to serve as your essential guide to understanding the basic grammar rules specific to spoken Jaffna Tamil, allowing you to communicate effectively and authentically. Here's how to make the most of this resource and enhance your learning experience:

1. Reference for Grammar:
Utilise this book as a comprehensive reference for understanding the core grammatical structures of spoken Jaffna Tamil. Each section is tailored to present the fundamentals in a clear and concise manner. As you encounter various concepts, feel free to revisit the relevant chapters whenever you need clarification or reinforcement.

2. Build Your Vocabulary:
While grammar is crucial, vocabulary is the bedrock of effective communication. Start with a foundational vocabulary list and consistently add new words and phrases you encounter in your studies or during conversations. I encourage you to

create a dedicated section in your notebook or a digital document to keep track of these words. Regularly reviewing and practicing these terms will help solidify them in your active vocabulary.

3. Speak, Speak, and Speak Some More:

The most significant advancement in your spoken Tamil will come from active practice. Speaking the language as much as possible is essential to developing fluency and confidence. Don't shy away from making mistakes; they are a natural part of the learning process. Embrace every chance to converse and express yourself in Tamil, whether with fellow learners or native speakers.

4. Connect with Native Speakers:

One of the best ways to improve your spoken Tamil is to find native speakers to practice with. Engage in conversations, join language exchange groups, or participate in community events. This real-life practice will allow you to experience the language in its natural context, enhancing your understanding of colloquialisms, intonations, and cultural nuances.

5. Engage with Tamil Media:

Immerse yourself in Tamil culture by consuming a variety of media. Watch Tamil movies, listen to music, follow social media accounts, and explore YouTube channels that focus on Jaffna Tamil. These resources not only enrich your vocabulary and comprehension but also provide insight into the cultural context surrounding the language.

6. Participate in Tamil Culture:

Learning a language goes hand in hand with understanding the culture from which it emerges. Explore Tamil festivals, culinary traditions, literature, and art. Engaging with culture deepens your connection to the language and provides context for your conversations, making them more meaningful.

7. Regular Review and Practice:

As with any language, consistency is key. Set aside regular time for review and practice. Incorporate a mix of grammar exercises, vocabulary building, and real-life speaking opportunities into your routine. By reinforcing what you have learned, you will make steady progress.

This book is not just a set of guidelines; it is your companion on the exciting journey of learning Jaffna Tamil. By utilising it as a reference for grammar, building your vocabulary, and engaging actively with the language and culture, you will find yourself becoming more comfortable and proficient in spoken Tamil. Remember, every small step you take brings you closer to fluency, and with patience and perseverance, success will be yours. Embrace the journey, and enjoy every moment of learning!

Gratitude & Acknowledgements

Dear Readers,

This book is a labor of love that wouldn't have come to fruition without the unwavering support and inspiration from my beloved grandparents, Ayiliam and Nagalingam. Growing up, I cherished every moment spent learning Tamil with them, as their passion for the language was contagious. After school, I would eagerly rush to my grandparents' house, where my grandmother and I would delve into the intricacies of Tamil. Her enthusiasm for the language kindled a fire within me, fueling my own passion for this beautiful tongue.

When both of my grandparents passed away in 2015, I felt an urgent need to carry on their legacy. This longing led to the creation of The Tamil Channel, where I began posting short videos to teach Tamil. In the wake of the COVID-19 pandemic, I found a renewed purpose in teaching Tamil online as many people reached out to learn spoken Tamil. If it weren't for those students, I might not have taken the commitment to teaching Tamil online as seriously as I did.

In the early stages of my YouTube journey, I turned to my old Tamil school text books for reference. However, as I progressed, I realised I needed further guidance on Tamil grammar. I am grateful for the knowledge and structure provided by M.A. Nuchman sir's book 'Basic Tamil Grammar' during my early teaching years. A heartfelt thank you also goes to Joseph Vilvaraj sir, who enriched my learning experience with additional resources during my BA Tamil course.

I want to extend my heartfelt thanks to all my students whose curiosity and enthusiasm for Tamil have inspired me to become a better learner and teacher. Your interest in the language has motivated me immensely, and I am especially grateful to those who helped me in transcribing spoken Tamil sounds—your contributions have been invaluable in making our lessons more engaging and effective. Thank you for your unwavering support and for being an essential part of this journey; I am honoured to learn and grow alongside you.

I am eternally grateful to my biggest cheerleader, my little sister Anukiraha. Your support from the very first video posted on YouTube to this moment has been invaluable.

In closing, I would like to extend my sincere thanks to my husband, Umeswaran, for the countless hours spent proofreading my work. Your unwavering enthusiasm and thoughtful responses to my spontaneous, often serious, questions about Tamil truly reflect your dedication. I couldn't have done this without your support.

I hope this book serves as a valuable resource for all who wish to learn and appreciate the beauty of spoken Jaffna Tamil.

With heartfelt gratitude,

U. N. Sabthaswaraja
Tamil Language Centre

1. Introduction to Tamil Letters

The Tamil script is a complex and vibrant writing system composed of 247 distinct characters, arranged within a framework known as 'nedungkanakku'. It includes 12 vowels, 18 consonants, 216 compound letters, and a special character.

Contemporary Tamil also incorporates grantha letters - though they are not officially recognised within the standard Tamil script, they play a significant role in transcribing words borrowed from other languages.

Tamil letters can be categorised into two main groups: primary and secondary. The primary letters comprise the 12 vowels and 18 consonants, serving as the foundational sounds of the language. Conversely, the secondary letters include the 216 compound letters and the special character ௲.

This chapter will delve into the structure and classification of Tamil letters, providing key insights into their function and significance within the language.

Primary Letters
12 vowels & 18 consonants

Secondary Letters
216 compound letters & 1 special character

Auxiliary Characters

Auxiliary characters do not possess independent phonetic values but rather serve as integral components of compound letters, augmenting the vowel sounds they accompany.

Tamil Nedungkanakku

ஃ	அ	ஆ	இ	ஈ	உ	ஊ	எ	ஏ	ஐ	ஒ	ஓ	ஔ
க்	க	கா	கி	கீ	கு	கூ	கெ	கே	கை	கொ	கோ	கௌ
ங்	ங	ஙா	ஙி	ஙீ	ஙு	ஙூ	ஙெ	ஙே	ஙை	ஙொ	ஙோ	ஙௌ
ச்	ச	சா	சி	சீ	சு	சூ	செ	சே	சை	சொ	சோ	சௌ
ஞ்	ஞ	ஞா	ஞி	ஞீ	ஞு	ஞூ	ஞெ	ஞே	ஞை	ஞொ	ஞோ	ஞௌ
ட்	ட	டா	டி	டீ	டு	டூ	டெ	டே	டை	டொ	டோ	டௌ
ண்	ண	ணா	ணி	ணீ	ணு	ணூ	ணெ	ணே	ணை	ணொ	ணோ	ணௌ
த்	த	தா	தி	தீ	து	தூ	தெ	தே	தை	தொ	தோ	தௌ
ந்	ந	நா	நி	நீ	நு	நூ	நெ	நே	நை	நொ	நோ	நௌ
ப்	ப	பா	பி	பீ	பு	பூ	பெ	பே	பை	பொ	போ	பௌ
ம்	ம	மா	மி	மீ	மு	மூ	மெ	மே	மை	மொ	மோ	மௌ
ய்	ய	யா	யி	யீ	யு	யூ	யெ	யே	யை	யொ	யோ	யௌ
ர்	ர	ரா	ரி	ரீ	ரு	ரூ	ரெ	ரே	ரை	ரொ	ரோ	ரௌ
ல்	ல	லா	லி	லீ	லு	லூ	லெ	லே	லை	லொ	லோ	லௌ
வ்	வ	வா	வி	வீ	வு	வூ	வெ	வே	வை	வொ	வோ	வௌ
ழ்	ழ	ழா	ழி	ழீ	ழு	ழூ	ழெ	ழே	ழை	ழொ	ழோ	ழௌ
ள்	ள	ளா	ளி	ளீ	ளு	ளூ	ளெ	ளே	ளை	ளொ	ளோ	ளௌ
ற்	ற	றா	றி	றீ	று	றூ	றெ	றே	றை	றொ	றோ	றௌ
ன்	ன	னா	னி	னீ	னு	னூ	னெ	னே	னை	னொ	னோ	னௌ

1.1. Vowels

Tamil features a total of **12 vowels**, which can be categorised into two groups: short vowels and long vowels. Short vowels are referred to as kuRil in Tamil, while long vowels are known as neDil. To illustrate their duration, you can think of a click of a finger as a unit of measurement: short vowels are pronounced for the duration of one click, whereas long vowels are pronounced for the duration of two clicks.

அ	ஆ	இ	ஈ	உ	ஊ	எ	ஏ	ஐ	ஒ	ஓ	ஔ
a	aa	i	ii	u	uu	e	ee	ai	o	oo	au

Short vowels
அ இ உ எ ஒ

Long vowels
ஆ ஈ ஊ ஏ ஐ ஓ ஔ

Among the long vowels, ஐ and ஔ are classified as diphthongs. Diphthongs consist of a combination of two vowel sounds pronounced in a single syllable.

Rule: Vowel letters may only appear at the beginning of a word.

When a vowel sound is heard in the middle or at the end of a word, it is part of a compound letter. You will learn more about compound letters on page 7.

1.2. Consonants

In Tamil, there are **18 consonants**. Notably, each consonant is marked by a dot above it. In the accompanying table of consonants, some letters are represented in capital letters to signify retroflex sounds. You can learn more about retroflex sounds on page 21.

க்	ங்	ச்	ஞ்	ட்	ண்	த்	ந்	ப்
k	ng	ch	nj	D	N	th	ndh	p

ம்	ய்	ர்	ல்	வ்	ள்	ழ்	ற்	ன்
m	y	r	l	v	L	L	t	n

Rule: Consonant letters may only appear in the middle or at the end of a word.

When a consonant sound is heard at the beginning of a word, it is part of a compound letter.

Consonants are categorised into 3 groups based on their pronounced sound: Vallinam, Idaiyinam and Mellinam.

Vallinam - Hard Consonants - க் ச் ட் த் ப் ற்

Vallina consonants are characterised by their hard plosive sounds. These consonants, along with their compound letters, occur more frequently in Tamil words compared to medium or soft consonants. Mastering the accurate pronunciation of these six consonants is essential. Additionally, compound letters of vallina consonants exhibit allophonic variations. You can learn more about allophones on page 22.

Idaiyinam - Medium Consonants - ய் ர் ல் வ் ள் ழ்

Idai in Tamil means in-between. Hence idaiyina consonants are medium sounds between the hard vallina consonants and the soft mellina consonants.

Note: In spoken Tamil, the retroflex consonants ள் and ழ் are pronounced identically. However, in written Tamil, there is a distinction between the two sounds. The use of either ள் or ழ் can change the meaning of a word, so it is important to recognise and understand which consonant is used in each case, despite their similar pronunciation in spoken Tamil.

Mellinam - Soft Consonants - ங் ஞ் ண் ந் ம் ன்

Mellina consonants are characterised as soft or nasal sounds. These consonants are typically followed by their corresponding compound letters or, more commonly, by their buddy compound letters. You will notice that each of the soft consonants is paired with a compound letter of a hard consonant. These letter combinations of soft & hard sounds appear together in words.

consonant	compound letters of	examples
ங்	க்	தங்கச்சி, வாங்கோ
ஞ்	ச்	இஞ்சி, செஞ்சனான்
ண்	ட்	கண்டி, மண்டை
ந்	த்	வந்தவா, சந்தி
ம்	ப்	சம்பல், பாம்பு
ன்	ற்	நன்றி, கன்று

1.3. Compound Letters

In Tamil, compound letters are formed by combining consonants and vowels. When a consonant is paired with a vowel, it creates a unique letter known as a compound letter. Combining the **18 consonants** and the

7

12 vowels, results in **216 compound letters**. Note that not all of these combinations are in active use.

To effectively learn compound letters, it is essential to first familiarise yourself with the 12 vowels and 18 consonants. Understanding these foundational elements will significantly ease the process of learning compound letters.

How to Construct Compound Letters
The order of combining consonants and vowels is crucial.

Rule: Consonant + Vowel = Compound Letter

In this structure, the consonant sound always precedes the vowel sound.

Example:
Combining consonant + vowel results in a compound letter:
க் + அ = க

If you reverse the order, where the vowel is placed before the consonant, the combined sound remains the same:
அ + க் = அக்

Let's take the consonant க் (k) as an example, and see how it can be combined with each of the 12 vowels to form compound letters.

க் + அ = க	க் + எ = கெ
க் + ஆ = கா	க் + ஏ = கே
க் + இ = கி	க் + ஐ = கை
க் + ஈ = கீ	க் + ஒ = கொ
க் + உ = கு	க் + ஓ = கோ
க் + ஊ = கூ	க் + ஔ = கௌ

Looking at the compound letters of க், what do you notice? The compound letters maintain the basic structure of the consonant க், with distinct modifications introduced for each vowel.

In general, the compound letters of the vowels உ and ஊ present a notable exception to this pattern. Unlike other vowel combinations, the compound letters of உ and ஊ exhibit three distinct variations, showcasing greater diversity among their corresponding compound forms.

1.4. Auxiliary Characters

Auxiliary characters, also called helper characters, are added to compound letters. These characters do not have independent phonetic values; they function as essential parts of compound letters, representing the vowel sounds.

Refer to the table below, which illustrates the characters added to the main body of the compound letters for all the vowel sounds. In this table, the square symbolises the core structure of the consonant, excluding the dot. This also represents the compound letters of the vowel அ.

அ		எ	
ஆ		ஏ	
இ		ஐ	
ஈ		ஒ	
உ		ஓ	
ஊ		ஔ	

The compound letters for உ and ஊ incorporate one of three specific characters that are appended to the primary structure of the letter.

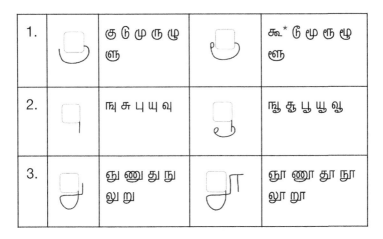

There is a consistent pattern in the formation of the compound letters of உ and ஊ, with the exception of கூ, which does not conform to this pattern. Additionally, note the similarities between compound letters of ஆ and compound letters of ஊ (category 3).

ஆ ஞா ணா தா நா லா றா
ஊ ஞூ ணூ தூ நூ லூ றூ

It is noteworthy that not all compound letters are actively utilised in Tamil. Refer to the table below, where the letters shaded in gray denote those that are either seldom used or infrequently encountered in the language.

ஃ	அ	ஆ	இ	ஈ	உ	ஊ	எ	ஏ	ஐ	ஒ	ஓ	ஔ
க்	க	கா	கி	கீ	கு	கூ	கெ	கே	கை	கொ	கோ	கௌ
ங்	ங	ஙா	ஙி	ஙீ	ஙு	ஙூ	ஙெ	ஙே	ஙை	ஙொ	ஙோ	ஙௌ
ச்	ச	சா	சி	சீ	சு	சூ	செ	சே	சை	சொ	சோ	சௌ
ஞ்	ஞ	ஞா	ஞி	ஞீ	ஞு	ஞூ	ஞெ	ஞே	ஞை	ஞொ	ஞோ	ஞௌ
ட்	ட	டா	டி	டீ	டு	டூ	டெ	டே	டை	டொ	டோ	டௌ
ண்	ண	ணா	ணி	ணீ	ணு	ணூ	ணெ	ணே	ணை	ணொ	ணோ	ணௌ
த்	த	தா	தி	தீ	து	தூ	தெ	தே	தை	தொ	தோ	தௌ
ந்	ந	நா	நி	நீ	நு	நூ	நெ	நே	நை	நொ	நோ	நௌ
ப்	ப	பா	பி	பீ	பு	பூ	பெ	பே	பை	பொ	போ	பௌ
ம்	ம	மா	மி	மீ	மு	மூ	மெ	மே	மை	மொ	மோ	மௌ
ய்	ய	யா	யி	யீ	யு	யூ	யெ	யே	யை	யொ	யோ	யௌ
ர்	ர	ரா	ரி	ரீ	ரு	ரூ	ரெ	ரே	ரை	ரொ	ரோ	ரௌ
ல்	ல	லா	லி	லீ	லு	லூ	லெ	லே	லை	லொ	லோ	லௌ
வ்	வ	வா	வி	வீ	வு	வூ	வெ	வே	வை	வொ	வோ	வௌ
ழ்	ழ	ழா	ழி	ழீ	ழு	ழூ	ழெ	ழே	ழை	ழொ	ழோ	ழௌ
ள்	ள	ளா	ளி	ளீ	ளு	ளூ	ளெ	ளே	ளை	ளொ	ளோ	ளௌ
ற்	ற	றா	றி	றீ	று	றூ	றெ	றே	றை	றொ	றோ	றௌ
ன்	ன	னா	னி	னீ	னு	னூ	னெ	னே	னை	னொ	னோ	னௌ

Instead of trying to memorise all the compound letters at once, focus on learning the most frequently used letters first. Here's a suggestion:

1. Learn the vowels and consonants first.
2. Learn the auxiliary characters.
3. Learn the compound letters of உ & ஊ
4. Practice reading simple words or children's stories to get a feel for how compound letters are used in context.

You'll quickly notice that not all compound letters are used in Tamil, making it easier to learn and remember the ones that are most relevant. By following this approach, you'll be able to learn the Tamil script more efficiently and effectively.

1.5. Special Character ஃ

The letter ஃ is a distinctive symbol in Tamil, classified separately from both vowels and consonants. Its usage in contemporary Tamil is relatively rare, and it is often visually represented as three dots or circles. The pronunciation of ஃ corresponds to a **ch** sound, represented in the International Phonetic Alphabet (IPA) as [x].

This letter typically appears in the middle of words, situated between a short vowel sound and a vallina compound letter. For example:

அஃது
இஃது

In contemporary spoken Tamil, ஃ has taken on new functions. When combined with the letter ப or its compound forms, it produces the **f** sound. While **f** is not a native sound in Tamil, it has been incorporated into the language through loanwords from other languages. Some examples include:

phone = ஃபோன்
Fatima = ஃபாத்திமா

1.6. Grantha Letters

Historically, Grantha letters were used to represent sounds in Sanskrit that are not inherently present in the Tamil language. The use of Grantha letters allows Tamil speakers to transcribe Sanskrit (and other foreign) words accurately, especially in religious, literary, or academic contexts. Nowadays, grantha letters can be found in many Tamil (Sanskrit derived) names.

These are the most frequently used grantha letters in contemporary Tamil. The first 4 Grantha letters are consonants. These can be combined with Tamil vowels to form compound letters.

ஸ்	ஜ்	ஷ்	ஹ்ற	ஸ்ரீ
s	j	sh	h	shrii

ஸ்ரீ is a grantha compound letter made up of ஸ் + ர் + ஈ. The term ஸ்ரீ signifies auspiciousness or respect in Tamil. It is commonly found in temples and Hindu scriptures, serving as a mark of reverence. Additionally, ஸ்ரீ is often incorporated into Tamil names that have their roots in Sanskrit, such as ஸ்ரீப்ரியா (Shripriya) or ஸ்ரீராம் (Shreeram). This letter reflects cultural and spiritual significance within the Tamil language, highlighting the rich interconnection between Tamil and Sanskrit traditions.

Grantha letters are utilised in Tamil primarily to represent sounds that do not have direct equivalents in the native Tamil script. This is particularly true for words borrowed from other languages, especially Sanskrit.

For instance, the Grantha consonant ஸ் is commonly used, as it represents the s sound, which is not naturally found among Tamil consonants. However, in instances where Tamil has its own compound letters to express similar sounds, such as ச (sa), we tend to favor these native representations.

As a result, while Grantha letters serve an important role in accommodating foreign sounds, their usage is typically reserved for cases where the Tamil script lacks an appropriate alternative. This ensures a more accurate and phonetic transcription of borrowed words while maintaining the integrity of the Tamil language.

Grantha Compound letters

	அ	ஆ	இ	FF	உ	ஊ	எ	ஏ	ஐ	ஒ	ஓ	ஔ
ஜ்	ஜ	ஜா	ஜி	ஜீ	ஜு	ஜூ	ஜெ	ஜே	ஜை	ஜொ	ஜோ	ஜௌ
ஸ்	ஸ	ஸா	ஸி	ஸீ	ஸு	ஸூ	ஸெ	ஸே	ஸை	ஸொ	ஸோ	ஸௌ
ஷ்	ஷ	ஷா	ஷி	ஷீ	ஷு	ஷூ	ஷெ	ஷே	ஷை	ஷொ	ஷோ	ஷௌ
ஹ்	ஹ	ஹா	ஹி	ஹீ	ஹு	ஹூ	ஹெ	ஹே	ஹை	ஹொ	ஹோ	ஹௌ

2. Sounds

This chapter examines the phonetic structure of Tamil, focusing on the sound changes that characterise this language. Tamil is notable not only for its extensive literary tradition but also for its distinct phonological features. A key aspect of Tamil phonetics is its use of retroflex sounds, which are relatively uncommon in many other languages and contribute to the unique articulation of Tamil.

The analysis also encompasses changes in vowel sounds that play a significant role in the language's phonetic inventory. Attention is given to the concept of allophones and how these subtle variations influence pronunciation and meaning. Understanding these phonetic phenomena provides deeper insights into the linguistic complexities of Tamil and the ways in which sound patterns inform its structure and usage.

2.1. ற் vs ந் Sound Variations

The consonants ந் and ற் are pronounced differently as consonants and compound letters.

The consonant ந் is pronounced differently depending on whether it functions as a standalone consonant or as part of compound letters.

When pronounced as a consonant, ந் is articulated by touching your front teeth with the tip of your tongue (see diagram 1). In contrast, the compound letters formed from ந் are pronounced as an **n** sound, which is identical to that of the consonant ன். To pronounce the **n** sound correctly, the tip of the tongue should touch the alveolar ridge (see diagram 2). Although ந and ன are phonetically identical, understanding the context in which each compound letter is used is vital.

Diagram 1   Diagram 2

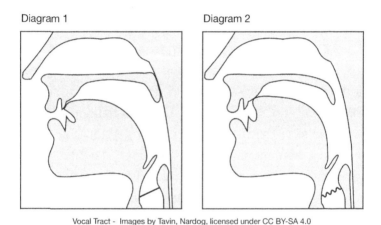

Vocal Tract - Images by Tavin, Nardog, licensed under CC BY-SA 4.0

Compound letters of ந்: Only appear at the beginning of a word.

Examples:

நாய் (naay)

நன்றி (nanRi)

நில்லுங்கோ (nillunggoo)

Compound letters of ன்: Only appear in the middle or at the end of a word.

Examples:

என்ன (enna)

வானம் (vaanam)

பனி (pani)

To illustrate, let's examine the word நான் (naan). Both **n** sounds in நான் are pronounced identically. Following the rules: நான் = நா is at the beginning of the word and ன் is at the end. While these rules generally apply, there are exceptions where compound letters of ந் can appear in the middle of a word. For example, in compound words like தேநீர் (theeniir) or in names such as அபிநயா (Abinayaa).

The consonant ற் is pronounced as a **t** sound when it appears in isolation within a word. This sound is produced by pressing the tip of the tongue against the alveolar ridge (see diagram 3).
Examples:

சிற்பம் (sitpam)

பயிற்சி (payitchi)

In contrast, when compound letters of ற் are found in isolation in a word, they are pronounced as a rolled **R** sound. To achieve this pronunciation, the tongue must be rolled, making contact with the underside of the tip and rolling from the back of the alveolar ridge to the front (see diagram 3).

Examples:

கறி (kaRi)

சுறா (suRaa)

Diagram 3

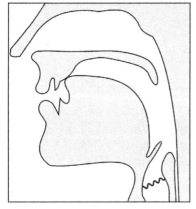

Vocal Tract - Image by Tavin, Nardog, licensed under CC BY-SA 4.0

2.2. Retroflex Sounds

Retroflex sounds in Tamil are produced by curling the tongue and pressing the underside of the tip of the tongue against the post alveolar region (see image below).

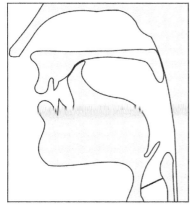

Vocal Tract - Image by Tavin, Nardog, licensed under CC BY-SA 4.0

In addition, it's important to keep the sides of your tongue flat against the inner edges of your gum line while producing retroflex sounds. These sounds are characterised by a deeper resonance created in the middle and back of your mouth.

To locate the post-alveolar region, follow these steps:

1. Start with the tip of your tongue positioned just behind your front teeth and gently trace along your gum line.

2. You will encounter a small flat area (alveolar ridge) followed by a slight upward curve (alveolar arch).
3. After the alveolar arch, gum will level out (hard palate).
4. To produce retroflex sounds in Tamil, position the bottom tip of your tongue where your gum line begins to level off before the hard palate.

When articulating retroflex compound letters, ensure that your tongue rolls forward from the post-alveolar region towards the alveolar ridge.

There are 5 retroflex sounds in Tamil:

ட் ண் ழ் ள் ற்*

While ற is considered a retroflex sound, only the compound letters of ற produce retroflex sounds. The consonant ற் is pronounced as a **t** sound as in cat, put or sit.

2.3. Allophones

An allophone refers to a variation of the same letter or phoneme that produces different sounds. In Tamil, compound letters of vallina consonants exhibit allophonic variations. This means that the pronunciation of these compound letters can change depending on their position in a word or the surrounding letters. It's important to note that allophone rules can vary significantly by region. The rules covered in this book apply to spoken Jaffna Tamil.

All compound letters of the 6 vallina consonants below have allophones.

க் ச் ட் த் ப் ற்

It is crucial to pay close attention to the allophones of க் and ச், as they can produce a diverse range of sounds that differ from their original consonantal forms. In contrast, the compound letters ட், த், ப், and ற் typically exhibit just two types of allophones, which correspond to either a hard or soft pronunciation.

Allophones of க்

The rules apply to all compound letters of க். Remember, the consonant sounds remain the same and are not affected by these rules.

Pronunciation: *k*
Rule: Compound letters of க் appear at the beginning of a word. Examples: கண், காது, கிளி
Rule: Compound letters of க் appear after the consonant க். Examples: அக்கா, மூக்கு, வெக்கம்

Pronunciation: *h*
Rule: Compound letters of க் appear after a vowel or compound letter. Examples: தாகம், முகில், வாகனம்
Rule: Compound letters of க் appear after the consonants ய் ர் ல் ழ் ள்.   Examples: நாய்கள், மார்கழி, கொள்கை

Pronunciation: *g*
Rule: Compound letters of க் appear after the consonant ங். Examples: தங்கச்சி, மூங்கில், அரங்கம்

Example:

    The word காகங்கள் (crows) is made of 3 different compound letters of க். Each one of them is pronounced differently. கா-கங்-கள் is romanised as kaa-hang-gaL. The first letter of the word, கா, is pronounced as *kaa*, because it is at the beginning of the word. The letter க in the second syllable is pronounced as *ha*, because the letter appears after a compound letter. Finally, the third க letter in the third syllable is pronounced as *ga,* because க appears after the consonant ங்.

Allophones of ச்

All rules apply to all compound letters of ச்.

Pronunciation: **ch**
Rule: Compound letters of ச் appear after the consonants ச் or ற். Examples: பச்சை, மூச்சு, பயிற்சி

Pronunciation: **s**
Rule: Compound letters of ச் appear at the beginning of a word. Examples: சப்தா, சீனி, சிவப்பு
Rule: Compound letters of ச் appear after a vowel or compound letter. Examples: மாசி, பாசம், வாசி

Pronunciation: **j**
Rule: Compound letters of ச் appear after the consonant ஞ். Examples: இஞ்சி, மஞ்சள், குஞ்சு

Example 1:

 The word சஞ்சிகை (magazine) has two compound letters of ச். சஞ்சிகை is romanised as sanj-ji-hai. The first letter, ச, is pronounced as *sa*, because ச is at the beginning of the word. சி is pronounced *ji*, because it appears after the consonant ஞ்.

Example 2:

Let's break down the word **சிவப்புச்சட்டை** into syllables. சி-வப்-புச்-சட்-டை = si-vap-puch-chaD-DTai. The first compound letter சி is pronounced *si*, because it appears at the beginning of a word. ச in the fourth syllable is pronounced *cha*, because it appears after the consonant ச் in the word.

Allophones of ட்

Compound letters of ட் either have a soft or hard pronunciation based on their neighbouring letters. The default sound of ட (Da) is soft. When compound letters of ட் appear after the consonant ட், the compound letters are pronounced hard. Regardless of how soft or hard the letters are pronounced, remember that ட் and all of its compound letters are retroflex sounds.

Pronunciation: **hard ட் (DT)**
Rule: Compound letters of ட் appear after the consonant ட். Examples: வட்டம், சட்டை, குட்டி

Pronunciation: **soft ட் (D)**
Rule: Compound letters of ட் appear after a vowel or compound letter. Examples: நாடி, பாடு, சாடி
Rule: Compound letters of ட் appear after the consonant ண். Examples: சண்டை, வண்டு, கண்டி

Example:

     The word கட்டடம் (kaD-DTa-Dam) has two ட letters, each pronounced slightly differently. The first ட is pronounced hard, because the compound letter appears after the consonant ட். The second ட is pronounced soft, because the compound letter appears after a vowel.

     Don't worry if you find it difficult to distinguish between the soft and hard sounds at first. The differences are subtle, and it often requires time and practice to become familiar with them.

Allophones of த்

     Compound letters of த் have a soft and hard pronunciation. The hard pronunciation of த for example, can also be described as sharp **th**. The soft pronunciation of த can be described as a soft **dh** sound. For both sounds, the tip of your tongue should still be between both sets of teeth.

Pronunciation: hard த் (th)
Rule: Compound letters of த் appear at the beginning of a word. Examples: தம்பி, திங்கள், தாங்கோ
Rule: Compound letters of த் appear after the consonant த். Examples: தாத்தா, பத்து, சித்தி

Pronunciation: soft த் (dh)
Rule: compound letters of த் appear after a vowel or compound letter. Examples: காதல், பதில், கதவு
Rule: compound letters of த் appear after the consonant ந். Examples: பந்து, பந்தல், சந்தி

Example:

In the word சந்தித்தேன் (sandh-dhith-theen) there are 2 compound letters of த், each pronounced differently. தி is pronounced soft as **dhi**, because the compound letter appears after the consonant ந். தே is pronounced sharp as **thee**, because it appears after the consonant த்.

Allophones of ப

Compound letters of ப் can be pronounced hard as **pa** sound or soft as a **ba** sound. The default pronunciation of ப is **pa**.

28

Pronunciation: hard ப - *pa*
Rule: Compound letters of ப் appear at the beginning of a word. Examples: பாசம், புட்டு, பூச்சி
Rule: Compound letters of ப் appear after the consonant ப். Examples: அப்பா, தொப்பி, கப்பல்

Pronunciation: soft ப - *ba*
Rule: Compound letters of ப் appear after a vowel or compound letter. Examples: கோபம், உபசரிப்பு, கோபுரம்
Rule: Compound letters of ப் appear after the consonants ம் ன் ய் ர் ல் ள் ழ். Examples: அன்பு, சம்பல், மார்பு

Example:

The word பேரின்பம் (pee-rin-bam) contains two compound letters of ப். பே is pronounced as *pee*, because it appears at the beginning of the word. ப in the last syllable is pronounced *ba*, because it follows the consonant ன்.

Allophones of ற்

The consonant ற் is pronounced as a *t* sound when it appears in isolation in a word. It usually appears in the middle of a word followed by compound letters of க், ச் or ப். Compound letters of ற் that appear in isolation in a word are pronounced as rolled *R* sounds: ற (Ra), றா (Raa), றி (Ri), றீ (Rii). When ற் is followed by its own compound letter, it is not pronounced as a rolled *R* sound, but rather as a flat *t* sound.

Pronunciation: ற் (*t*)
Rule: Consonant ற் is followed by compound letters of க் ச் ப். Examples: கற்கள், முயற்சி, சிற்பம்

Pronunciation: ற்ற (*t*)
Rule: Consonant ற் is followed by compound letters of ற். Examples: காற்று, மற்ற, நெற்றி

Pronunciation: ற (rolled *R*)
Rule: compound letters of ற் appear after a vowel or compound letter. Examples: கறி, புறா, வறுவல்
Rule: compound letters of ற் appear after the consonant ன். Examples: நன்றி, கன்று, சென்றாள்

2.4. Vowel Sound Changes

Tamil vowel sounds can vary based on their surrounding letters. Tamil vowels and compound letters produce different vowel sounds when they are followed by retroflex sounds.

அ ஆ

The default pronunciation for அ and ஆ are mid-open *a* sounds. For example, in words such as cup or gut. Vowels or compound letters of அ & ஆ followed by retroflex sounds are pronounced with a more open *a* sound. When pronouncing retroflex sounds, the tip of the tongue needs to curl back, which requires you to open your mouth wider.

Try saying out the words below row by row. Can you hear the difference in the vowel sounds preceding the retroflex sounds?

1.	அன்னம்	அண்ணா
2.	ஆதி	ஆடி
3.	கல்	கள்
4.	வால்	வாழ்
5.	கரி	கறி

இ ஈ எ ஏ

The rules governing the sound changes for இ, ஈ, எ, and ஏ are consistent. When these vowels appear before retroflex sounds, they take on a distinct *eu* sound, similar to the **i** sound in the English word **bird**. This is also referred to as the schwa sound, a neutral, relaxed pronunciation where the tongue is not elevated and the mouth remains relatively closed.

Try pronouncing the word pairs:

இலை	இடை
கிலி	கிழி

ஈரம்	ஈழம்
சீலை	சீடை

எரி	எறி
தெரிவு	தெளிவு

ஏன்	ஏழு
பேன்	பேண்

உ

The vowel உ and its compound letters are pronounced differently based on their position in a word and neighbouring letters. உ and all of its compound letters are either pronounced with protruded lips as in **foot** or **book** or as a schwa sound *eu* as in **bird**.

Pronunciation: protruded உ
Rule: Words starting with vowel/compound letter of உ. Examples: உள்ளி, குட்டி

Pronunciation: protruded உ
Rule: Word starting with the letter உ or its compound letter, immediately followed by a compound letter of உ. Examples: உடும்பு, முருகன்

Pronunciation: lazy உ (*eu*)
Rule: Compound letters of உ appearing in the middle or at the end of a word. Examples: அம்பு, இருமல்

Example 1:

குடும்பம் (ku-Dum-bam) contains 2 different compound letters of உ. கு is pronounced with **protruded lips**, because it appears at the beginning of the word. டு is also pronounced with **protruded lips**, because it appears after the compound letter of உ.

Example 2:

The word உடுப்பு (u-Dup-peu) consists of multiple உ sounds. உ is pronounced with **protruded lips**, because it appears at the beginning of the word. டு is also pronounced with **protruded lips**, because it appears after the உ sound. பு is pronounced as a lazy eu sound, because it appears in the middle of a word, and not following an உ sound.

3. Building Blocks of Tamil Sentences

In this chapter, you will explore the fundamental building blocks of the Tamil language by examining its four main categories of words. Understanding these classifications is essential for grasping sentence structure and enhancing your linguistic proficiency.

1. Nouns: These words identify people, places, things, or concepts, serving as the subjects and objects within sentences.

2. Verbs: Verbs express actions, occurrences, or states of being, playing a crucial role in conveying meaning and driving narratives.

3. Affixes and Particles: This category includes prefixes, suffixes and words that modify or connect other words, enriching the language with nuance and precision.

4. Adjectives and Adverbs: These words enhance comprehension by describing nouns and verbs, adding detail and clarity to expressions.

By delving into each of these categories, we will gain a deeper understanding of how they interact within sentences, providing a strong foundation for mastering Tamil grammar.

3.1. Nouns

In Tamil, nouns are classified into two categories: rational and irrational. Rational nouns refer to entities that possess intellect or higher consciousness, such as deities and human beings. Irrational nouns, on the other hand, encompass animals and inanimate objects. This classification is particularly significant when it comes to third-person and plural pronouns, as it influences how these pronouns are used in sentences.

Refer to the table below for a clearer representation of these classifications:

Rational Pronouns		Irrational Pronouns	
she	அவள் / அவா	it	அது
he	அவன் / அவர்		
they	அவெ	they	அதுகள்

An important distinction in Tamil lies in the use of third-person plural pronouns. When referring to a group of people, the pronoun அவெ is used, while அதுகள் is employed for a group of animals or objects. This distinction is not only significant in terms of pronouns but also plays a crucial role in verb conjugation, as person suffixes are added to verbs based on these classifications.

In spoken Tamil, you may occasionally hear native speakers use அதுகள் when discussing a group of people. This is not a mistake; rather, it is an intentional choice that conveys disrespect, as irrational beings are perceived as lower in status than humans. Therefore, using irrational pronouns in reference to individuals can signal a lack of respect.

Pluralisation in Tamil

In general, nouns can be pluralised by adding the suffix **-கள்** to the end of the noun.

Examples:
>   மாணவர்கள் (students)
>   வீடுகள் (houses)
>   குடும்பங்கள் (families)
>   கடைகள் (shops)

Exception: Rational nouns that denote personal relationships are pluralised using the suffix **-மார்**.

Examples:
>   அம்மாமார் (mothers)
>   அப்பாமார் (fathers)
>   அக்காமார் (older sisters)
>   தம்பிமார் (younger brothers)

Note on pluralising irrational nouns

In spoken Tamil, -கள் suffix is sometimes omitted by speakers in irrational form.

Examples:

The phrase 'கண்ணெ மூடுங்கோ' translates to 'Close [your] eyes'. However, a more literal translation of this sentence would be 'Close the eye'. This does not imply that only one eye needs to be closed; rather, it refers to closing both eyes collectively.

Similarly, 'கையெ கழுவுங்கோ' literally means 'Wash the hand'. Yet, this expression is not limited to washing just one hand; it encompasses washing both hands.

This illustrates how plural irrational nouns in spoken Tamil are often expressed in singular form.

Understanding Nouns and Adjectives in Tamil

Nouns and adjectives function differently in Tamil than they do in English, which can sometimes lead to misunderstandings for beginners. For instance, the English sentence 'It is cold here' translates to 'இங்கெ குளிர்' in spoken Tamil. A common misconception in this context is to interpret 'cold' as an adjective, assuming it translates to குளிர். In reality, however, குளிர் is a noun meaning 'coldness'.

3.2. Verbs

Tamil verbs can seem daunting at first, but fear not! While the complexity of verb conjugation may feel overwhelming initially, our step-by-step guide will help make this essential aspect of the Tamil language more manageable.

In Tamil, verbs are inherently more complex than in English. A complete verb consists of a verb stem followed by various suffixes that convey information about tense and the subject of the action. In essence, a complete verb provides context about when the action occurs and who is performing it.

Key Components of Tamil Verbs:

1. Verb Stem: The base form of the verb.

2. Suffixes: These are added to the verb stem to indicate:
   2.1. Tense: When the action is taking place (e.g., past, present, future).
   2.2. Person: Who is performing the action (e.g., first person, second person, third person).
   2.3. Conditional Forms: These indicate the circumstances under which an action occurs.

39

Complete vs. Incomplete Verbs

Verbs can be classified as complete or incomplete. Only a complete verb can form a full sentence, while incomplete verbs serve specific functions within a larger conjugation. For example, they might indicate ongoing actions or be part of compound actions that express multiple events in one expression.

Examples:
சாப்பிட்டு முடிச்சிட்டென்
(I have finished eating)

சாப்பிட்டு கொண்டு குடிச்சனான்
(I drank while I was eating)

To deepen your understanding, refer to our dedicated chapter on verbs, where you will learn to identify the various components of a verb and how to effectively conjugate them. With practice, you'll find that mastering Tamil verbs is not only achievable but also rewarding!

3.3. Grammatical Particles

Just as nouns and verbs form the foundation of a sentence, grammatical particles are equally important. They serve to connect different elements of a sentence, enhancing clarity and coherence. Learning these connecting words and affixes is essential for mastering Tamil, as they help indicate relationships between ideas and provide important details about actions and subjects.

Key Components:

1. Affixes:
These include various grammatical modifiers that change the meaning of root words.

2. Conjunctions:
These words, such as and, or, but, and despite link thoughts and clauses together.

3. Prepositions:
Indicate locations, time, and other relational contexts.

3.4. Articles

Grammatical articles are not as commonly used or as complex in Tamil as in languages like English. Tamil primarily uses nouns, pronouns, and demonstratives to indicate specificity. However, the concept of definiteness and indefiniteness can be conveyed through certain words and structures.

1. Definite Article: In Tamil, the definite article 'the' is usually implied rather than explicitly stated. For example, சாதாரண வீடு means the ordinary house. The article 'the' is understood through context. In some cases, the accusative case suffix எ can be used to convey the meaning of the definite article 'the' in English. This often signifies a specific object in a sentence. For example: புத்தகத்தெ தாங்கோ, which translates to 'give (me) the book'.

2. Indefinite Article: The indefinite article 'a' or 'an' can be implied by using the word ஒரு, which means 'one' or 'a'. For example, ஒரு நாய் translates to 'a dog'.

3. Demonstrative Pronouns: Words like இந்த (this) and அந்த (that) can also convey a sense of specificity similar to articles in English.

While Tamil does not have grammatical articles in the same way that English does, it effectively uses context and specific words to convey the same meanings.

3.5. Adjective & Adverbs

Nouns can be modified using specific suffixes to create adjectives and adverbs. Adjectives are words that describe nouns. Adverbs are words that describe verbs or actions. Adding the suffix -ஆன forms adjectives, while the suffix -ஆ forms adverbs.

Examples:

noun	-ஆன (adjective)	-ஆ (adverb)
நீலம்	நீலமான	நீலமா
வடிவு	வடிவான	வடிவா
குளிர்	குளிரான	குளிரா

3.6. Connecting Letters

When adding suffixes to Tamil words, the ending of the word may change or additional letters may need to be added to ensure a smooth transition in pronunciation. This section outlines some basic principles of connecting letters, particularly useful for understanding grammatical cases and conjunctions.

General Principles

1. Letter Modifications: Some suffixes may require changes at the end of the root word when attached. These changes often occur to maintain fluidity in sound.

2. Suffixes Starting with Vowels: Most suffixes begin with a vowel sound. However, in spoken Tamil, these vowel sounds are sometimes omitted, which can affect how we attach suffixes.

3. Consonant Endings: When a word ends with a consonant and a consonant suffix is added, the original form of the suffix (starting with a vowel) should be used instead.

Examples:

When using the suffix -க்கு (which means 'to'), it can typically be added directly to the end of a word, especially if the word ends with a vowel.

அம்மா + -க்கு = அம்மாக்கு (to mother)

However, if the word ends with a consonant, it is necessary to return to the original form of the suffix, which in this case would be -உக்கு.

அம்மன் + -உக்கு = அம்மனுக்கு (to Amman)

It's important to note that there may be exceptions, particularly for words ending in the letter ம், but for the purpose of this guide, we focus on these foundational principles. As you progress in your study of Tamil, you will discover more nuances and rules to navigate effectively.

	ending of word	connecting letter
1	consonant	consonant+vowel
2	ம்	த்த்
3	அ/ஆ/உ/ஊ/ஒ/ஓ	வ்
4	இ/ஈ/எ/ஏ/ஐ	ய்

Rules for Grammatical Cases:

1. word ends in consonant sound
   = consonant + suffix
   அம்மன் + எ = அம்மனெ

2. word ends in ம் = word -ம் + த்த் + suffix
   புத்தகம் + எ = புத்தக+த்த்+எ = புத்தகத்தெ

3. word ends in அ/ஆ/உ/ஊ/ஒ/ஓ = word + வ் + suffix
   அம்மா + எ = அம்மா + வ் + எ = அம்மாவெ

4. word ends in இ/ஈ/எ/ஏ/ஐ = word + ய் + suffix
   தம்பி + எ = தம்பி + ய் + எ = தம்பியெ

Rules for உம் suffix rules:

1. word ends in consonant sound
   = consonant + suffix
   அம்மன் + உம் = அம்மனும்

2. word ends in ம் = word + suffix
   புத்தகம் + உம் = புத்தகமும்

3. word ends in அ/ஆ/உ/ஊ/ஒ/ஓ = word + வ் + suffix
   அம்மா + உம் = அம்மா + வ் + உம் = அம்மாவும்

4. word ends in இ/ஈ/எ/ஏ/ஐ = word + ய் + suffix
   தம்பி + உம் = தம்பி + ய் + உம் = தம்பியும்

Exception to the Rule:

While the general principles of connecting letters in Tamil grammar provide a solid foundation for attaching suffixes, there are exceptions that are worth noting. One such exception involves words that end with the sound உ when the suffix -உம் is added.

When a word ends with an உ sound and the suffix -உம் is added, in spoken Tamil, for ease of pronunciation, one of the உ sounds is often omitted, resulting in a more streamlined version: உப்பு + உம் = உப்பும். This simplification makes the spoken form more fluid and natural.

46

3.7. Tamil Sentence Structure

Tamil sentences are structured in a Subject-Object-Verb (SOV) format, contrasting with English's Subject-Verb-Object (SVO) structure. Simple Tamil sentences can be constructed just using complete verbs.

Examples:

போனான். (I went.)

சாப்பிடுவா. (She will eat.)

An important rule to note in Tamil is that verbs always come at the end of a sentence. Typically, the subject is followed by the object, but this order is flexible due to suffixes that indicate the relationship between the nouns and the verb.

Consider the sentence: அம்மா அக்காவோட போறா, which translates to 'Mother is going with big sister'. We can rearrange it without changing the meaning: அக்காவோட அம்மா போறா, meaning 'With big sister, mother is going'.

In both sentences, the meaning remains the same: it is the mother who is going with the big sister. This consistency in meaning despite shifts in word order is due to the suffix -ஒட indicating 'with', which clarifies the relationship.

Now, if we swap the subjects in the English sentence, 'Big sister is going with mother', the meaning changes completely. This highlights how Tamil relies on suffixes for clarity, allowing for flexibility in sentence structure.

An additional aspect of Tamil is that sentences may occasionally lack verbs, particularly the verb 'to be'. In Tamil, verbs such as உண்டு, ஆகும், and இருக்கு to convey the concept of existence or being. However, the verb 'is/am' is often implied and not explicitly stated.

For example:

> என்ர பெயர் சப்தா: My name [is] Sabtha.
> நான் சப்தா: I [am] Sabtha.

In both examples, the verb 'is/am' is understood but not expressed.

4. Introduction to Tamil Verbs

In the Tamil language, the distinction between spoken and written forms is particularly pronounced in verbs. While nouns tend to maintain their form across different variations of Tamil, verb endings can differ significantly from one region to another. This variation in verb conjugation is one of the key differences that can be observed among Tamil speakers worldwide.

This book is focused on teaching grammar for spoken Jaffna Tamil. By exploring the verb conjugations that are prevalent in this region, you will gain insights that are not only applicable to Jaffna Tamil but also provide you with the foundational principles that can be generalised to both written Tamil and other regional variations.

With a solid grasp of these verb structures, you will be better equipped to navigate the nuances of spoken Tamil and enhance your ability to communicate effectively in a variety of contexts.

Tamil verbs often carry a reputation for their complexity, and this perception is not without merit. However, the good news is that mastering Tamil verbs is entirely achievable through a clear understanding of some fundamental principles. In this chapter, you will explore the essential components that make up Tamil verbs, including their structure, verb stems, and the various suffixes used in conjugation.

You will learn how to effectively conjugate verbs by combining these elements, allowing you to communicate actions across different contexts. The infinitive form and the AvP form of verbs, which are crucial for creating compound verbs and conditional verbs are also reviewed. Additionally, you will learn how to express negations, expanding your ability to articulate different meanings and scenarios.

By the end of this chapter, you'll have a solid foundation in spoken Tamil verbs, equipping you with the skills needed to communicate more effectively and confidently in everyday conversations.

4.1. Structure of the Verb

A complete verb in Tamil consists of a verb stem followed by a series of suffixes, typically including at least one tense suffix and one person suffix. Without these components, a verb cannot be classified as complete. However, it's essential to recognise the importance of incomplete verbs as well. While they may not convey meaning on their own, when combined with complete verbs, they can form continuous or compound verbs.

Let's examine the basic components of a complete verb:

Verb Stem + Tense Suffix + Person Suffix

Adding suffixes to the verb stem can be more intricate than this straightforward formula. Depending on the specific verb stem ending or the class of the verb, certain modifications may occur. For example, some verb stems may change from a long vowel sound to a short vowel sound when suffixes are appended. To streamline the learning process, the tense and person suffixes have been consolidated into a single combined suffix while also identifying the necessary verb stem changes according to the tense.

In the following sections, you will find a table detailing various verb stems based on tense, along with four tables of suffixes categorised by tense and person. Understanding these different components will provide you with a solid foundation for conjugating your own verbs.

In this book, the following five tenses are presented to enhance your understanding and usage of verbs in Tamil:
1. Simple Past Tense: I went
2. Present Progressive Tense: I am going
3. Simple Present Tense: I go
4. Simple Future Tense: I will go
5. Intentional Future Tense: I am going to go

It's important to highlight that the Simple Future Tense is not as commonly utilised in spoken Tamil as it is in English. Instead, native speakers often use the Present Progressive Tense when discussing future actions or opt for the Intentional Future Tense. We will delve deeper into these nuances, particularly in the context of compound verbs, later in the book.

Verb Classes

In Tamil, verbs can be classified into two categories: strong verbs and weak verbs. This classification is significant because the suffixes that are added to these verbs change depending on their type. However, for your convenience, suffixes have been combined already, allowing you to focus on learning without needing to distinguish between verb classes at this stage.

At this point in your journey, understanding the distinction between strong and weak verbs is not a primary concern. The only instance where verb classes become critical is when conjugating verbs in the future tense, specifically for the irrational form, அது. To assist you, strong verbs are clearly marked with an asterisk in the tables, and you'll find them in the first half of the provided list.

4.2. Verb Stems

The verb stem serves as the foundational element of any verb, encapsulating the action it represents. In this book, the 20 most frequently used verbs have been selected for their relevance and commonality in everyday conversation. These verb stems not only convey essential actions but can also function as command verbs, representing the imperative form of the verb. It's important to note that the commands derived from these stems are informal. When addressing individuals, always opt for the formal command variations, which will be detailed in the dedicated verbs section. Verb stems that are marked with an asterisk indicate strong verbs, while those without an asterisk denote weak verbs.

Verb stems

1	இரு*	sit/wait
2	குடி*	drink
3	நில்*	stand/wait
4	குடு*	give (3rd)
5	பார்*	look/see
6	கதை*	talk
7	கேள்*	ask/listen
8	நட*	walk
9	சமை*	cook
10	வை*	put/place
11	எடு*	take
12	வா	come
13	போ	go
14	சாப்பிடு	eat
15	தா	give (1st/2nd)
16	செய்	do
17	சொல்	say
18	காட்டு	show
19	போடு	put on/throw
20	ஓடு	run

Tense based verb stems

verb stem	English	simple past	present continuous	simple present	simple future
இரு*	sit/wait	இருந்த	இருக்கி	இருக்கிற	இருப்
குடி*	drink	குடிச்ச	குடிக்கி	குடிக்கிற	குடிப்
நில்*	stand/wait	நிண்ட	நிக்கி	நிக்கிற	நிப்
குடு*	give (3rd)	குடுத்த	குடுக்கி	குடுக்கிற	குடுப்
பார்*	look/see	பாத்த	பாக்கி	பாக்கிற	பாப்
கதை*	talk	கதைச்ச	கதைக்கி	கதைக்கிற	கதைப்
கேள்*	ask/listen	கேட்ட	கேக்கி	கேக்கிற	கேப்
நட*	walk	நடந்த	நடக்கி	நடக்கிற	நடப்
சமை*	cook	சமைச்ச	சமைக்கி	சமைக்கிற	சமைப்
வை*	put/place	வச்ச	வைக்கி	வைக்கிற	வைப்
எடு*	take	எடுத்த	எடுக்கி	எடுக்கிற	எடுப்
வா	come	வந்த	வா	வாற	வருவ்
போ	go	போன	போ	போற	போவ்
சாப்பிடு	eat	சாப்பிட்ட	சாப்பிடு	சாப்பிடுற	சாப்பிடுவ்
தா	give (1st & 2nd)	தந்த	தா	தாற	தருவ்
செய்	do	செஞ்ச	செய்யி	செய்யிற	செய்வ்
சொல்	say	சொன்ன	சொல்லு	சொல்லுற	சொல்லுவ்
காட்டு	show	காட்டி(ன)	காட்டு	காட்டுற	காட்டுவ்
போடு	put on/ throw	போட்ட	போடு	போடுற	போடுவ்
ஓடு	run	ஓடின	ஓடு	ஓடுற	ஓடுவ்

4.3. Suffixes and Pronouns

Understanding suffixes and pronouns is essential for mastering verb conjugation in Tamil. First and foremost, you'll need to familiarise yourself with Tamil pronouns, which play a crucial role in sentence construction and verb conjugation. For a comprehensive list of pronouns, please refer to page 76 of this book.

To simplify your learning experience, straightforward lists of suffixes have been compiled, which combine both tense suffixes and person suffixes into a single suffix. It's important to note that the irrational plural pronoun (அதுகள்) has been omitted, as it is used infrequently in everyday conversations.

Simple past tense suffixes

நான்	-னான்
நீ	-னீ
நீங்கள்	-னீங்கள்
அவா	-வா
அவள்	-வள்
அவர்	-வர்
அவன்	-வன்
அது	-து
நாங்கள்	-னாங்கள்
அவெ	-வெ

Present progressive tense suffixes

நான்	-றென்
நீ	-றே
நீங்கள்	-றீங்கள்
அவா	-றா
அவள்	-றாள்
அவர்	-றார்
அவன்	-றான்
அது	-து
நாங்கள்	-றம்
அவெ	-னம்

Simple present tense suffixes

நான்	-னான்
நீ	-னீ
நீங்கள்	-னீங்கள்
அவா	-வா
அவள்	-வள்
அவர்	-வர்
அவன்	-வன்
அது	-து
நாங்கள்	-னாங்கள்
அவெ	-வெ

Simple future tense suffixes

நான்	-வென் - பென்
நீ	-வே -பே
நீங்கள்	-வீங்கள் - பீங்கள்
அவா	-வா
அவள்	-வாள்
அவர்	-வார்
அவன்	-வான்
அது	-க்கும்* - உம்
நாங்கள்	-வம் -பம்
அவெ	-வினம் -பினம்

How to Conjugate a Verb:

Once you have familiarised yourself with the verb stems and suffixes, you can easily combine them to form complete verbs.

For example, if you want to say 'I went':

1. Identify the past tense stem for the verb go: போன

2. Find the past tense suffix for first person: -னான்

Now, combine them:
போன + னான் = போனனான்

It's that simple!

Remember: The verb is/am does not exist in Tamil.

1. My name is Sabtha = என்ர பெயர் சப்தா
2. She is Nila = அவா நிலா
3. He is hungry = அவருக்கு பசிக்கிது

4.4. Commands

The polite command form is the default command form. Command verbs are useful in daily conversations.

	English	verb stem	polite command	negative command
1	sit wait	இரு*	இருங்கோ!	இருக்காதைங்கோ
2	drink	குடி*	குடியுங்கோ	குடிக்காதைங்கோ
3	stand wait	நில்*	நில்லுங்கோ	நிக்காதைங்கோ
4	give (3rd pers)	குடு*	குடுங்கோ	குடுக்காதைங்கோ
5	look see	பார்*	பாருங்கோ	பாக்காதைங்கோ
6	talk	கதை*	கதையுங்கோ	கதைக்காதைங்கோ
7	ask	கேள்*	கேளுங்கோ	கேக்காதைங்கோ
8	walk	நட*	நடவுங்கோ	நடக்காதைங்கோ
9	cook	சமை*	சமையுங்கோ	சமைக்காதைங்கோ
10	put place	வை*	வையுங்கோ	வைக்காதைங்கோ

	English	verb stem	polite command	negative command
11	take	எடு*	எடுங்கோ	எடுக்காதைங்கோ
12	come	வா	வாங்கோ	வராதைங்கோ
13	go	போ	போங்கோ	போகாதைங்கோ
14	eat	சாப்பிடு	சாப்பிடுங்கோ	சாப்பிடாதைங்கோ
15	give (1st/?nd)	தா	தாங்கோ	தராதைங்கோ
16	do make	செய்	செய்யுங்கோ	செய்யாதைங்கோ
17	say	சொல்	சொல்லுங்கோ	சொல்லாதைங்கோ
18	show	காட்டு	காட்டுங்கோ	காட்டாதைங்கோ
19	throw put on	போடு	போடுங்கோ	போடாதைங்கோ
20	run	ஓடு	ஓடுங்கோ	ஓடாதைங்கோ

4.5. Incomplete Verbs

Incomplete verbs lack an ending suffix to indicate person or tense, making them unsuitable for use in standalone sentences. However, they play a crucial role in forming compound and conditional verbs. In this book, we will focus on two types of incomplete verbs: the infinitive form and the adverbial participle (AvP).

To effectively create compound verbs, it's important to understand both the infinitive form and the AvP form of verbs. The infinitive form can be combined with a complete verb to create the continuous tense. AvPs are utilised in both continuous and compound verbs.

Incomplete Verbs

	English	verb stem	infinitive	AvP
1	sit/wait	இரு*	இருக்க	இருந்து
2	drink	குடி*	குடிக்க	குடிச்சு
3	stand/wait	நில்*	நிக்க	நிண்டு
4	give (3rd pers)	குடு*	குடுக்க	குடுத்து
5	look/see	பார்*	பாக்க	பாத்து
6	talk	கதை*	கதைக்க	கதைச்சு
7	ask	கேள்*	கேக்க	கேட்டு
8	walk	நட*	நடக்க	நடந்து
9	cook	சமை*	சமைக்க	சமைச்சு
10	put/place	வை*	வைக்க	வச்சு
11	take	எடு*	எடுக்க	எடுத்து
12	come	வா	வர	வந்து
13	go	போ	போக	போய்
14	eat	சாப்பிடு	சாப்பிட	சாப்பிட்டு
15	give (1st/2nd)	தா	தர	தந்து
16	do	செய்	செய்ய	செஞ்சு
17	say	சொல்	சொல்ல	சொல்லி
18	show	காட்டு	காட்ட	காட்டி
19	put on/throw	போடு	போட	போட்டு
20	run	ஓடு	ஓட	ஓடி

4.6. Compound Verbs

Compound verbs consist of at least two verbs working together. In cases where the verbs express continuous actions, there will be a main (action) verb alongside an auxiliary (helper) verb. When two actions are completed simultaneously, the structure usually includes one incomplete verb followed by a complete verb.

Example:

நான் சாப்பிட போறென். Here, சாப்பிட is the action verb, but it's incomplete as it lacks tense/person suffixes. போறென் is a complete verb meaning 'I'm going'. In this context, it functions as the auxiliary verb, indicating the intentional future tense.

Compound verbs can also express two actions occurring simultaneously or sequentially.

Example 1:

நான் போய் சாப்பிடுறென். In this sentence, போய் (go) is the incomplete verb, while சாப்பிடுறென் is the complete verb meaning 'I'm eating'. Together, they indicate that I am going first, then eating, showing two actions completed one after the other.

Example 2:

நான் சாப்பிட்டு கொண்டு படம் பாக்கிறென். Here, சாப்பிட்டு is the incomplete verb, followed by கொண்டு, which is a continuous tense marker, and பாக்கிறென்,

meaning 'I am watching'. The complete sentence translates to: I'm watching a film while eating. The inclusion of கொண்டு indicates that both actions are happening simultaneously.

4.7. Negations

In Tamil, negations can be added to a sentence by appending இல்லெ at the end of the verb. The negation form varies depending on the tense of the verb.

For the simple future tense, the conjugated form of 'மாட்-' (meaning 'will not') is used to negate verbs. To form the correct negation, you need to take the stem 'மாட்-' and add the appropriate person suffix based on the subject.

In spoken Jaffna Tamil, when you add இல்லெ to the infinitive form of a verb, the last letter of the infinitive often changes. For example:

சாப்பிட + இல்லெ = சாப்பிடேல்லெ

Here, the last letter of சாப்பிட merges with இ, resulting in ஏ when pronounced together.

Summary of Negation Rules:

1. Negations for simple past and present progressive tenses use the same form.
2. The negation form for simple future is based on the stem 'ᴅᴨL-' plus the appropriate person suffix.
3. We have created a table for easy reference, showing the conjugated negation forms.
4. Negations are consistent (except for simple future tense) regardless of the person and do not require a suffix to indicate the subject.

Verb Negations

verb stem	English	simple past / present progressive	simple present	simple future	going to future
இரு	sit wait	இருக்கேல்லெ	இருக்கிறேல்லெ	இருக்க மாட்-	இருக்கப் போறேல்லெ
குடி	drink	குடிக்கேல்லெ	குடிக்கிறேல்லெ	குடிக்க மாட்-	குடிக்கப் போறேல்லெ
நில்	stand wait	நிக்கேல்லெ	நிக்கிறேல்லெ	நிக்க மாட்-	நிக்கப் போறேல்லெ
குடு	give (3rd)	குடுக்கேல்லெ	குடுக்கிறேல்லெ	குடுக்க மாட்-	குடுக்கப் போறேல்லெ
பார்	look see	பாக்கேல்லெ	பாக்கிறேல்லெ	பாக்க மாட்-	பாக்கப் போறேல்லெ
கதை	talk	கதைக்கேல்லெ	கதைக்கிறேல்லெ	கதைக்க மாட்-	கதைக்கப் போறேல்லெ
கேள்	ask	கேக்கேல்லெ	கேக்கிறேல்லெ	கேக்க மாட்-	கேக்கப் போறேல்லெ
நட	walk	நடக்கேல்லெ	நடக்கிறேல்லெ	நடக்க மாட்-	நடக்கப் போறேல்லெ
சமை	cook	சமைக்கேல்லெ	சமைக்கிறேல்லெ	சமைக்க மாட்-	சமைக்கப் போறேல்லெ
வை	put place	வைக்கேல்லெ	வைக்கிறேல்லெ	வைக்க மாட்-	வைக்கப் போறேல்லெ

Verb Negations

verb stem	English	simple past / present progressive	simple present	simple future	going to future
எடு	take	எடுக்கேல்லெ	எடுக்கிறேல்லெ	எடுக்க மாட்-	எடுக்கப் போறேல்லெ
வா	come	வரேல்லெ	வாறேல்லெ	வர மாட்	வரப் போறேல்லெ
போ	go	போகேல்லெ	போறேல்லெ	போக மாட்-	போகப் போறேல்லெ
சாப்பிடு	eat	சாப்பிடேல்லெ	சாப்பிடுறேல்லெ	சாப்பிட மாட்-	சாப்பிடப் போறேல்லெ
தா	give (1st/2nd)	தரேல்லெ	தாறேல்லெ	தர மாட்-	தரப் போறேல்லெ
செய்	do	செய்யேல்லெ	செய்யிறேல்லெ	செய்ய மாட்-	செய்யப் போறேல்லெ
சொல்	say	சொல்லேல்லெ	சொல்லுறேல்லெ	சொல்ல மாட்-	சொல்லப் போறேல்லெ
காட்டு	show	காட்டேல்லெ	காட்டுறேல்லெ	காட்ட மாட்-	காட்டப் போறேல்லெ
போடு	put on throw	போடேல்லெ	போடுறேல்லெ	போட மாட்-	போடப் போறேல்லெ
ஓடு	run	ஓடேல்லெ	ஓடுறேல்லெ	ஓட மாட்-	ஓடப் போறேல்லெ

Person suffixes for future simple negations

நான்	-மாட்டென்
நீ	-மாட்டே
நீங்கள்	-மாட்டீங்கள்
அவா	-மாட்டா
அவள்	-மாட்டாள்
அவர	-மாட்டார்
அவன்	-மாட்டான்
அது	-மாட்டுது
நாங்கள்	-மாட்டம்
அவெ	-மாட்டினம்

Negating Sentences Without Verbs

In Tamil, the verb 'is' or 'am' is often implied and not explicitly stated in sentences.

For instance:

நான் தமிழ். (I am Tamil.)

Negating such sentences is straightforward. By simply adding இல்லெ at the end of the sentence, you can negate it:

நான் தமிழ் இல்லெ. (I am not Tamil.)

It's important to note that இல்லெ does not only translate to 'no', but it also conveys the meaning of 'not'.

Example:
அவா ஒரு அம்மா. (She is a mother.)

Negating this sentence would be:
அவா ஒரு அம்மா இல்லெ. (She is not a mother.)

4.8. Conditional Tense

The conditional suffix -ஆல் is used to convert verbs into the conditional tense, allowing you to express hypothetical situations or conditions. To create the conditional tense, add the -ஆல் suffix to the AvP verb form. It's important to note that when doing this, the final vowel sound of the verb stem is typically dropped. The consonant sound at the end of the verb then merges with the vowel sound of the suffix.

Examples:

சாப்பிட்டு + ஆல் = சாப்பிட்டால்

இருந்து + ஆல் = இருந்தால்

Negative Conditional Tense

To create a negative conditional tense in Tamil, you add the suffix -ஆட்டில் to the infinitive verb. In this process, the infinitive verb drops its final vowel, allowing the ending consonant to merge with the vowel of the suffix.

Examples:

சாப்பிட + ஆட்டில் = சாப்பிடாட்டில்
இருக்க + ஆட்டில் = இருக்காட்டில்

Note: In spoken Tamil, some speakers may simplify the pronunciation by omitting the 'ல்' sound at the end of the conditional form. As a result, they may say 'சாப்பிடாட்டி' instead of 'சாப்பிடாட்டில்'.

Sentence structure of conditional sentences

The structure of a conditional sentence places the conditional clause first, followed by the result in Tamil sentences. For example, 'நீங்கள் வந்தால், நான் சாப்பிடுவென்' translates to 'If you come, I will eat'. Unlike English, where you can begin the sentence with either the conditional or the result, Tamil requires that the conditional clause precedes the outcome to ensure clarity and coherence. This specific order is crucial for the sentence to make sense in Tamil.

4.9. Notes on verb usage

Verbs: தா vs. குடு

தா and குடு both translate to 'give' in English, but they are used in different contexts.

தா: This verb is employed specifically for the first and second person when they are the recipients. It is used when the speaker (first person) or the listener (second person) is receiving something.

Examples:

எனக்கு ஒரு பழம் தாங்கோ. (Give me a fruit.)

உங்களுக்கு ஒரு பழம் தாறென். (I'm giving you a fruit.)

குடு: This verb is used when giving something to a third person. It indicates an action where the receiver is not the speaker or the listener.

Examples:

நான் அம்மாக்கு ஒரு பழம் குடுத்தனான்.

(I gave mother a fruit.)

அம்மா அக்காக்கு ஒரு பழம் குடுத்தவா.

(Mother gave older sister a fruit.)

Verbs: இரு vs. நில்

இரு: This is a versatile verb that can mean sit, exist, be, live, have, or wait. Its default translation is 'to sit'. It conveys a sense of being in a particular location for a long-term duration or residing there.

நில்: This verb also has several meanings, including stand, stay and wait, with 'stand' as its default translation. It typically indicates a short-term stay or presence in a place.

Examples:

நான் கனடால இருக்கிறென். (I live in Canada)

நான் கனடால நிக்கிறென். (I am/I'm staying in Canada)

5.1. Pronouns

When applying case suffixes to subject pronouns, the stem undergoes changes for the first and second person. Here are the pronouns along with their stem changes:

நான்	என்
நாங்கள்	எங்கள்
நீ	உன்
நீங்கள்	உங்கள்

This chapter contains all the pronouns altered by the addition of case suffixes. For guidelines on when to use these pronouns, please refer to the section on grammatical cases on page 94.

A key point to remember is that formal pronouns are the default choice. Informal pronouns should only be used with individuals whom you are very close to, typically those who are younger than you. For instance, parents may use informal pronouns when addressing their children, while children should always employ formal pronouns when speaking to their parents or elders. When in doubt, it is best to opt for formal pronouns. In the tables provided, informal pronouns are indicated with *(inf)*.

Subject Pronouns

நான்	I		
நீ	you *(inf)*	நாங்கள்	we
நீங்கள்	you	நீங்கள்	you
அவள்	she *(inf)*	அவெ	they
அவா	she		
அவன்	he *(inf)*	அது	it
அவர்	he	அதுகள்	they

Object Pronouns

என்னெ	me		
உன்னெ	you *(inf)*	எங்களெ	us
உங்களெ	you	உங்களெ	you
அவளெ	her *(inf)*	அவெயெ	them
அவாவெ	her		
அவனெ	him *(inf)*	அதெ	it
அவரெ	him	அதுகளெ	them

Possessive Pronouns

Most possessive pronouns in Tamil conclude with the suffix **-ன்ர**. When pronouncing this suffix, please note that the character ர is articulated as a **t** sound rather than a soft **r** sound.

என்ர	my/mine		
உன்ர	your/yours *(inf)*	எங்கட	our/s
உங்கட	your/s	உங்கட	your/s
அவளின்ர	her/s *(inf)*	அவைவன்ர	their/s
அவான்ர	her/s		
அவன்ர	his *(inf)*	அதின்ர	its
அவற்ற	his	அதுகளின்ர	their/s

Instrumental Pronouns

என்னால	I'm able to		
உன்னால	you're able to *(inf)*	எங்களால	we're able to
உங்களால	you're able to	உங்களால	you're able to
அவளால	she's able to *(inf)*	அவெயால	they're able to
அவாவால	she's able to		
அவனால	he's able to *(inf)*	அதால	it is able to
அவரால	he's able to	அதுகளால	they're able to

Dative Pronouns I

These pronouns are used when the pronoun is the recipient of an action.

எனக்கு	to me		
உனக்கு	to you *(inf)*	எங்களுக்கு	to us
உங்களுக்கு	to you	உங்களுக்கு	to you
அவளுக்கு	to her *(inf)*	அவைக்கு	to them
அவாக்கு	to her		
அவனுக்கு	to him *(inf)*	அதுக்கு	to it
அவருக்கு	to him	அதுகளுக்கு	to them

Dative Pronouns II

These pronouns are used when the action is done for the benefit of the pronoun (receiver).

எனக்காக எனக்காண்டி	for me		
உனக்காக உனக்காண்டி	for you *(inf)*	எங்களுக்காக எங்களுக்காண்டி	for us
உங்களுக்காக உங்களுக்காண்டி	for you	உங்களுக்காக உங்களுக்காண்டி	for you
அவளுக்காக அவளுக்காண்டி	for her *(inf)*	அவைக்காக அவைக்காண்டி	for them
அவாக்காக அவாக்காண்டி	for her		
அவனுக்காக அவனுக்காண்டி	for him *(inf)*	அதுக்காக அதுக்காண்டி	for it
அவருக்காக அவருக்காண்டி	for him	அதுகளுக்காக அதுகளுக்காண்டி	for them

5.2. Demonstrative Pronouns

Tamil utilises three distinct demonstrative particles to indicate or specify objects and actions based on their proximity to the speaker:

- அ (a): Indicates that the object or action is distant from both the speaker and the listener.
- இ (i): Indicates that the object or action is close to the speaker.
- உ (u): Indicates that the object or action is near the listener but away from the speaker.

This principle can be generalised to all third-person pronouns. It is noteworthy that the demonstrative particle உ has largely fallen out of use in many other Tamil-speaking regions, and today, it is primarily preserved within Jaffna Tamil.

Additionally, the interrogative particle எ (e), is employed to form questions. When combined with pronouns, this particle creates interrogative pronouns that can be used to ask more specific questions.

Examples

1. அது உங்கட புத்தகம். That is your book.
Here, அது indicates that the book is located away from both speaker and listener.

2. இது உங்கட புத்தகம். This is your book.

In this case, **இது** shows that the book is close to the speaker.

3. உது உங்கட புத்தகம். That is your book.

உது refers to a book that is nearer to the listener but away from the speaker, creating a sense of distance from the speaker.

4. எது உங்கட புத்தகம்? Which one is your book?

This question asks for clarification about a specific book among others.

Specific Examples:

1. அவா என்ர அம்மா. That is my mother or She is my mother.

The use of **அவா** emphasises that the speaker's mother is not near either the speaker or the listener, highlighting her presence in a more distant context.

2. இவா என்னோட வாறா. She is coming with me.

Using **இவா** indicates that the person being referred to is next to the speaker, emphasising a close proximity.

3. எவா உங்கட அம்மா? Which one is your mother?

This question specifically asks about identifying the person's mother among a group, emphasising the reference to **அம்மா**.

Demonstrative Pronouns

அது *that*	இது *this*	உது *that*	எது? *which one?*
away from speaker and listener	near speaker	away from speaker, near listener	question
அவள் *she (inf)*	இவள் *she (inf)*	உவள் *she (inf)*	எவள் *which (inf)*
அவா *she*	இவா *she*	உவா *she*	எவா *which*
அவன் *he (inf)*	இவன் *he (inf)*	உவன் *he (inf)*	எவன் *which (inf)*
அவர் *he*	இவர் *he*	உவர் *he*	எவர் *which*
அவெ *they*	இவெ *they*	உவெ *they*	எவெ *which*

Demonstrative Particles Used with Question Words

In Tamil, demonstrative particles can be effectively combined with question words to convey location and context more clearly. Here are some examples:

1. அங்கெ ஒரு புத்தகம் இருக்கு. There is a book over there. **அங்கெ** indicates that the book is situated away from both the speaker and the listener.

2. இங்கெ ஒரு புத்தகம் இருக்கு. Here is a book. **இங்கெ** shows that the book is close to the speaker, emphasising its proximity.

3. உங்கெ ஒரு புத்தகம் இருக்கு. There is a book near you. **உங்கெ** refers to a book that is close to the listener but away from the speaker, highlighting a sense of distance from the speaker's perspective.

அங்கெ *there*	இங்கெ *here*	உங்கெ *there*	எங்கெ *where*	*location*
அப்ப *then*	இப்ப *now*	//	எப்ப *when*	*time*
அப்படி *that way*	இப்படி *this way*	உப்படி *that way*	எப்படி *how*	*manner of doing something*
அவ்வளவு *that much*	இவ்வளவு *this much*	உவ்வளவு *that much*	எவ்வளவு *how much*	*quantity*
அத்தன *that many*	இத்தன *this many*	//	எத்தின *how many*	*quantity*
அந்த *that one*	இந்த *this one*	உந்த *that one*	எந்த *which*	*specific object*

5.3. Reflexive Pronouns

Reflexive pronouns are used to refer back to the subject of a sentence, indicating that the action is performed by the subject on itself. The primary reflexive pronouns are:

1. தான் = self (singular)
2. தாங்கள் = selves (plural)

There is no distinction made between rational and irrational beings when using these pronouns. தான் and தாங்கள் can be modified using case suffixes to convey different meanings or nuances.

Reflexive Pronouns

	singular	plural
subject	தான்	தாங்கள்
object	தன்னெ	தங்களெ
possessive	தன்ர	தங்களின்ர
locative	தன்னில	தங்களில
ablative	தன்னில இருந்து	தங்களில இருந்து
dative I	தனக்கு	தங்களுக்கு
dative II	தனக்காக / தனக்காண்டி	தங்களுக்காக / தங்களுக்காண்டி
social	தன்னோட	தங்களோட
instrumental	தன்னால	தங்களால

Example:

- அவா தன்னெ சொல்லுறா.
  She means herself.
- அவர் தன்ர வீட்ட போறார்.
  He is going to his own house.
- அவெ தங்களுக்காக எடுக்கினம்.
  They are taking (it) for themselves.

6.1. Forming Questions - ஆ suffix

You can turn a statement into a question by adding the suffix -ஆ to the end of the verb or to certain nouns within the sentence. This method helps to highlight different elements of the sentence based on where the suffix is added.

1. Adding -ஆ to the verb:
   - Statement: நீங்கள் கடைக்கு போறீங்கள்.
     (You are going to the shop.)
   - Question: நீங்கள் கடைக்கு போறீங்க**ளா**?
     (Are you qoing tn tho ohup?)

2. Adding -ஆ to a noun:
   - Statement: நீங்கள் கடைக்கு போறீங்கள்.
     (You are going to the shop.)
   - Question: நீங்கள் கடைக்**கா** போறீங்கள்?
     (Are you going to the **shop**?)

3. Adding -ஆ to the subject:
   - Statement: நீங்கள் கடைக்கு போறீங்கள்.
     (You are going to the shop.)
   - Question: நீங்க**ளா** கடைக்கு போறீங்கள்?
     (Are **you** going to the shop?)

The placement of the -ஆ suffix dictates the focus of the question. You can emphasise different parts of the sentence by where you add the suffix, thus shifting the attention.

6.2. Question Words

In addition to the -ஆ suffix, you can also use question words to inquire about specific details. In Tamil, question words do not start a sentence; instead, they follow the subject. Standard Sentence: நீங்கள் என்ன செய்யிறீங்கள்? (What are you doing?). If you want to give more emphasis to 'what,' you might say: என்ன நீங்கள் செய்யிறீங்கள்? (WHAT are you doing?)

Important Rule

You must not use both a question word and the -ஆ suffix in the same sentence. The presence of one precludes the other. Thus, a sentence must either have a question word or the -ஆ suffix, but not both.

Question Words

ஆர்	who
என்ன	what
ஏன்	why
எங்கெ	where
எப்ப	when
எப்படி	how
எவ்வளவு	how much
எத்தினெ	how many

Question Words II

எது	which one
எந்த	which
எவ்வளவு தூரம்	how far
எவ்வளவு நேரம்	how long (short term)
எவ்வளவு காலம்	how long (long term)
எத்தினெ தரம்	how many times

6.3. எது vs எந்த

The question words **எது** and **எந்த** are both used in questions, but they serve different grammatical functions and are used in different contexts.

1. எது
Function: Interrogative Pronoun
Usage: Used to ask about a specific object or thing, often when referring to a singular item in a general context.

Example:
எது உங்கட புத்தகம்? (Which one is your book?)
Here, **எது** is used to inquire about a specific book among several options, without specifying the noun.

2. எந்த
Function: Interrogative Adjective
Usage: Used to ask about a specific noun and must always be accompanied by that noun. It refers to a selection or choice among a group.

Example:
எந்த புத்தகம் உங்கட? (Which book is yours?)
In this case, **எந்த** modifies the noun **புத்தகம்** and specifies that the question is about a particular book within a known group.

7. Grammatical Cases - வேற்றுமை

Grammatical cases are called வேற்றுமை (Veetrumai) in Tamil. Cases indicate the relationship between nouns and other words within a sentence, often reflecting the noun's function, such as subject, object, or possession. Each case has distinct suffixes that are added to nouns. For instance, the nominative case is commonly used to indicate the subject of a verb, thus telling us who or what is performing the action. Conversely, the accusative case marks the direct object, highlighting what or whom the action is directed towards. The use of grammatical cases allows for a more nuanced expression of meaning, enabling the speaker to convey complex relationships and actions with clarity. In Tamil, the position of words in a sentence may be flexible, as the meaning is often discerned from the case suffixes rather than word order. Overall, grammatical cases enhance communication by providing essential information about the relationships and functions of nouns within the linguistic structure.

In Tamil, there are nine grammatical cases, and the suffixes used for these cases can vary by region. Below are the nine grammatical cases as used in spoken Jaffna Tamil.

Refer to the chapter on connecting letters to learn the rules for adding suffixes to words.

7.1. Grammatical Case Suffixes

	வேற்றுமை Case	Suffix	Example
1	எழுவாய் Nominative	-	அம்மா வாறா. Mother is coming.
2	செயப்படு பொருள் Accusative	-எ	அக்கா அம்மாவெ கூப்பிடுறா. Big sister is calling mother.
3	உடைமை Genitive	-(இ)ன்ர	அம்மான்ர புத்தகம். Amma's book.
4	இட Locative	-(இ)ல -(இ)ட்ட	அம்மா வீட்டில நிக்கிறா. Amma is at home.
5	நீங்கல் Ablative	-(இ)ல இருந்து -(இ)ட்ட இருந்து	அம்மா வீட்டில இருந்து வாறா. Amma is coming from home.
6	கொடை Dative	-(உ)க்கு -(உ)க்காக -(உ)க்காண்டி	அம்மா கடைக்கு போறா. Amma is going to the shop.
7	உடன் நிகழ்ச்சி Social	-ஓட	அம்மா அப்பாவோட போறா. Mother is going with father.
8	கருவி Instrumental	-ஆல	அம்மாவாலெ அழுறென். I'm crying because of amma.
9	விளி Vocative	!	தம்பி = தம்பீ

7.2. Nominative case - எழுவாய் வேற்றுமை

The nominative case is a grammatical case used primarily for the subject of a sentence. It marks the subject of a verb. To find the subject of a sentence you could ask: Who/What is doing the action. The nominative case is reflected in subject pronouns (p. 77).

Example: அம்மா வாறா.

In this sentence, அம்மா is the subject of the sentence, because she is doing the action. The action in this sentence is வாறா.

7.3. Accusative case - செயப்படுபொருள் வேற்றுமை

The accusative case, also known as the object case, is a grammatical case used to mark the direct object of a verb. The primary function of the accusative case is to denote the direct object of a transitive verb—the noun or pronoun that receives the action. In Tamil, the accusative case suffix -எ is used to indicate the case. Since the word order is flexible in Tamil, indicating the object with the accusative case suffix retains the meaning of the sentence, even if the word order is changed. The accusative case is reflected in object pronouns (p. 78).

Example: அக்கா அம்மாவெ கூப்பிடுறா.

In this example, **அக்கா** is the subject of the sentence. The action is **கூப்பிடுறா**. The direct object of the sentence is **அம்மாவெ** - it is indicated by the accusative case suffix. To find the object of the sentence, ask: Who/what is being called. In this example, **அம்மா**.

Even if the subject and object of the sentence were rearranged to: அம்மாவெ அக்கா கூப்பிடுறா, the meaning remains the same because the object has been marked by the accusative case suffix.

7.4. Genitive case - உடைமை வேற்றுமை

The genitive case, also known as the possessive case, is a grammatical case used to indicate relationships between nouns, typically expressing possession. In spoken Tamil, the genitive is marked by the suffix **-ன்ர**. For nouns that end in a consonant, the suffix **-இன்ர** is appended instead. The genitive case is reflected in possessive pronouns (p. 79).

Examples:

1. அம்மான்ர புத்தகம். In this example, **அம்மா** possesses the book, denoted by the suffix -ன்ர.

2. அருளின்ற புத்தகம். In this instance, the word அருள் ends with the consonant ள். Therefore, the suffix -இன்ற is applied, transforming it into அருளின்ற.

3. அவன்ற புத்தகம்.Here, the word அவன் ends with the consonant ன். When the suffix -ன்ற is added, one of the ன் letters drops, resulting in அவன்ற.

7.5. Locative case - இட வேற்றுமை

The locative case is a grammatical case used to indicate the location where an action occurs. This is not restricted to physical spaces, and can include states of being, too. In English, position prepositions such as **in, on** or **at** may be used. Spoken Tamil uses two different suffixes to indicate location.

-ல	places
-ட்ட	people

Example 1:

நான் பள்ளில நிக்கிறென். I am at school.

Here the -ல suffix has been added to the noun **பள்ளி**, which indicates that the subject **நான்** is located at the school.

Example 2:

அம்மாட்ட வாங்கோ. Come to mother.

In this example, the suffix -ட்ட has been attached to the word **அம்மா**, treating **mother** as a destination where the listener is invited to come to.

Example 3:

I am at home.

Translating this sentence into spoken Tamil, நான் வீட்டில நிக்கிறென் is correct. However, in spoken Tamil speakers tend to say நான் வீட்ட நிக்கிறென். This exception only applies to வீடு = house/home.

7.6. Ablative case - நீங்கல் வேற்றுமை

The ablative case is a grammatical case used to indicate separation, source, or movement away from a location or state. In English, we may use words such as **from** or **of** to indicate the same meaning. Two different suffixes are used based on whether the suffix is added to a location or person.

-ல இருந்து	places
-ட்ட இருந்து	people

Example 1:

அம்மா வீட்டில/வீட்ட இருந்து வாறா. Mother is coming from home. In this example, **அம்மா** is moving away from the location **வீடு**.

Example 2:

நாங்கள் நித்திரைல இருந்து எழும்பினாங்கள். We woke up from sleep. In this example, the focus is not on physical separation from a location, but rather on the separation from a state of being, specifically, the state of **sleep**.

7.7. Dative case - கொடை வேற்றுமை

The dative case is a grammatical case used to indicate the indirect object of a verb, which is typically the recipient of an action or the beneficiary. In spoken Tamil, the suffix **-க்கு** is commonly used to indicate the receiver of an action or the beneficiary. It answers the questions **to whom?** or **for whom?** regarding the action. The suffixes **-க்காக** and **-க்காண்டி** may be used,to indicate that something is done for the benefit of the receiver. It conveys intentions beyond personal ownership, suggesting a broader purpose. The dative case is reflected in dative pronouns (p. 81).

Examples:

1. நான் அம்மாக்கு ஒரு புத்தகம் குடுத்தனான். I gave a book to mother. In this example, the dative case is indicated by the suffix **-க்கு** added to **அம்மா**. The dative case is used here because **அம்மா** is the recipient of the action of giving. This example shows that the action of giving is directed towards **அம்மா**.

2. நான் அம்மாக்காக ஒரு கவிதை எழுதினான். I wrote a poem for mother. In this example, the suffix **-க்காக** is added to **அம்மா**, indicating that the poem was specifically written for **mother**. Using the dative case suffix **-க்கு** could also convey a similar idea, but the suffix **-க்காக** explicitly emphasises the purpose of writing the poem, making it clear that it is intended for **mother**. This distinction

highlights the intention behind the action, enhancing the meaning of the sentence. Note: The suffix **-க்காண்டி** can be used interchangeably with the suffix **-க்காக**.

Locative vs. Dative Case in Tamil

Here are examples illustrating the differences between locative and dative case suffixes:

1. படத்தெ என்னட்ட தாங்கோ: Give the picture to me. In this instance, **என்னட்ட** functions as a locative, treating **நான்/என்** (I/my) as a location. The request implies that while I am receiving the picture, it is not primarily intended for me; rather, I am holding it on someone else's behalf.

2. படத்தெ எனக்கு தாங்கோ: Give the picture to me. Here, **எனக்கு** signifies a direct request for the picture to be given to me. The emphasis is on receiving the item personally, indicating that it is intended for my use.

3. படத்தெ எனக்காக தாங்கோ: Give the picture for me. In this case, **எனக்காக** means **for my sake** or **on my behalf**. This request suggests that you are asking for the picture not only for your benefit but potentially for a specific purpose or reason related to you.

Additional Uses of the Dative Case

The dative case serves several functions beyond indicating who is receiving something.

1. Indicating Age

Example: எனக்கு முப்பது வயசு. I am thirty years old.

2. Expressing a person's state or condition

Example: எனக்கு பசிக்கிது. I am hungry.

3. Expressing feelings or emotions

Example: எனக்கு மகிழ்ச்சியா இருக்கு. I feel happy.

4. Indicates preferences, desires, or necessities.

Example 1: எனக்கு மாம்பழம் விருப்பம். I like mangoes.

Example 2: எனக்கு சாப்பாடு வேணும். I want food.

Example 3: எனக்கு ஒரு துவாய் தேவை. I need a towel.

5. Expressing Possession

The dative case can be used with the verb இருக்கு to show possession.

Example: எனக்கு வேலை இருக்கு. I have work.

7.8. Social Case - உடன் நிகழ்ச்சி வேற்றுமை

The social case is a grammatical case used to indicate the relationship between two or more nouns, specifically highlighting the means or accompaniment by which an action is performed. In spoken Tamil, the suffix -ஓட is commonly used to denote **with whom** or **with what** an action is carried out. It is crucial that both nouns are involved in the action simultaneously.

Example 1:

அம்மா அப்பாவோட கடைக்கு போறா. Mother is going to the shop with Father. In this example, அம்மா is the subject of the sentence, performing the action of going alongside அப்பா at the same time.

Example 2:

நான் அம்மாவோட ஒரு படம் பாக்கிறென். I am watching a movie with Mother. Here, நான் is the subject who is watching a movie alongside அம்மா.

7.9. Instrumental Case - கருவி வேற்றுமை

The instrumental case is a grammatical case that indicates the means or instrument by which an action is performed. Additionally, it can express the reason behind a noun's action or denote the source material. In spoken Tamil, the suffix -ஆல is added to the noun that functions as the instrument or means in the action described by the verb. The instrumental case is reflected in instrumental pronouns (p. 80).

Example 1:

நான் என்ர கையால சாப்பிடுறென். I am eating with my hand. In this example, **கை** serves as the means through which the action of eating is carried out.

Example 2:

நான் அம்மாவால அழுறென். I am crying because of mother. In this case, **அம்மா** is the reason for the action of crying, demonstrating how the instrumental case indicates causation.

The instrumental case can also convey one's ability or inability to perform a specific action. To construct a sentence using the instrumental suffix, follow this format:

noun+instrumental suffix + infinitive + ஏலும்/ஏலாது

அம்மா+ஆல சாப்பிட ஏலும்.

அம்மாவால சாப்பிட ஏலும். Mother is able to eat.

Here **-ஆல** conveys the idea of capability, indicating that the subject has the ability to perform the action of eating.

7.10. Vocative Case - விளி வேற்றுமை

The vocative case is a grammatical case used to directly address or summon someone, specifically designed to capture the attention of a person or thing. In Tamil, the vocative case does not require additional suffixes; rather, it involves the inflection of the noun by modifying its ending, usually elongating it to convey emphasis or exclamation.

For instance, when calling out to someone, the noun மாமி changes to மாமீ to effectively garner attention. A speaker might say, **மாமீ, இங்கெ வாங்கோ!** meaning **Aunt, come here!** In this example, the subject is implied rather than explicitly stated. The full sentence could alternatively be expressed as, மாமீ, நீங்கள் இங்கெ வாங்கோ! meaning Aunt, you come here!

This unique feature of the vocative case allows speakers to engage directly and expressively with others.

8.1. Position Prepositions

Position prepositions indicate the location or position of an object in relation to another object. These prepositions can be used on their own or combined with the suffix -க்கு, which adds clarity to the relationship between two objects.

1. Position prepositions used independently: When used independently, position prepositions provide information about the location of an object.
Example: நான் மேல நிக்கிறென். (I am upstairs.)

2. Position Prepositions with the suffix -க்கு: When combined with the suffix -க்கு, position prepositions specify the location of an object in relation to another object, enhancing the contextual meaning.
Example: நான் வீட்டுக்கு மேல நிக்கிறென்.
(I am on top of the house.)

Differences in Translation

It is important to note that the meaning of the sentences may vary slightly when translated into English due to the nuances of the Tamil language. In Tamil, the context is often more explicit, while English may convey similar meanings with different structures.

Position Prepositions with Examples

1	மேல up / upstairs / above	மேல பாருங்கோ. Look up.
	-க்கு மேல above / on top of	வீட்டுக்கு மேல பாருங்கோ. Look on top of the house.
2	கீழ down / below	கீழ வையுங்கோ. Put [it] down.
	-க்கு கீழ below / under	மேசைக்கு கீழ வையுங்கோ. Put [it] under the table.
3	வெளீல outside	அம்மா வெளீல நிக்கிறா. Amma is outside.
	-க்கு வெளீல outside of	அம்மா வீட்டுக்கு வெளீல நிக்கிறா. Amma is outside [of] the house.
4	உள்ள inside	உள்ள வாங்கோ. Come inside.
	-(உ)க்குள்ள inside of	கடைக்குள்ள வாங்கோ. Come inside the shop.
5	பக்கத்தில next to/near	பக்கத்தில நில்லுங்கோ. Stand next to / near.
	-க்கு பக்கத்தில next to/near	எனக்கு பக்கத்தில நில்லுங்கோ. Stand next to me.

6	கிட்ட near/close	கிட்ட வந்து இருங்கோ. Come and sit near.
	-க்கு கிட்ட near/close	அவாக்கு கிட்ட போய் இருங்கோ. Go and sit near her.
7	முன்னால in front	முன்னால வாங்கோ! Come in front.
	-க்கு முன்னால in front of	மரத்துக்கு முன்னால நிக்கிறார். He is standing in front of the tree.
8	பின்னால behind/back	அவா பின்னால இருக்கிறா. She's behind/She's sitting at the back.
	-க்கு பின்னால behind	அவா உங்களுக்கு பின்னால இருக்கிறா. She is sitting behind you.
9	இடைல in between	இடைல வையுங்கோ. Put it in between.
	-க்கு இடைல in between	புத்தகங்களுக்கு இடைல வையுங்கோ. Put it in between the books.
10	நடுவில in the middle	அவர் நடுவில இருக்கிறார். He is sitting in the middle.
11	சுத்தி around / surrounding	என்ர வீட்டெ சுத்தி ஓடினான். I ran around my house.

8.2. தான் - Emphatic Marker

The particle **தான்** serves as an emphatic marker in Tamil. It is placed after the specific element you wish to emphasise, and it can be translated into English as **only**, **just** or **indeed**.

Examples:

1. நான் பால் குடிக்கிறென்.
I am drinking milk.

2. நான் தான் பால் குடிக்கிறென்.
The emphasis here is on **I**.
I am the one drinking milk.

3. நான் பால் தான் குடிக்கிறென்.
Here, the focus shifts to **milk**.
I am just drinking milk, nothing more.

4. நான் பால் குடிக்கிறென் தான்.
In this case, the emphasis is on **drinking**.
I am drinking milk, so what?

These examples showcase how **தான்** can add different layers of meaning to a sentence by emphasising specific elements, especially in spoken Tamil.

8.3. எண்டு - Quotative Marker

In spoken Tamil, the particle எண்டு serves two significant functions: it acts as a **quotative marker** and as an **onomatopoeic marker.**

1. Quotative Marker:

When expressing an opinion, thought, or quoting someone, எண்டு connects the verb with what is being said or thought. In English, this is often conveyed using the relative particle **that.**

Examples:

'தண்ணி குடியுங்கோ' எண்டு அம்மா சொன்னவா.
(Amma said, 'Drink water'.) Here, எண்டு links the action of speaking to the quoted statement.

இது நீலம் எண்டு நான் நினைக்கிறென். (I think (that) this is blue.) In this sentence, எண்டு connects the thought with the assertion about the color.

2. Onomatopoeic Marker:

எண்டு also serves as an onomatopoeic marker when imitating sounds of actions, much like words such as **boom** or **bang** in English. It vividly captures the essence of certain sounds.

Examples:

'படக்' எண்டு விழுந்தவர்.

Here, 'padak' imitates the sound of the fall, indicating he fell suddenly or quickly.

'மடமட' எண்டு தண்ணியெ குடிக்கிறா.

In this sentence, மடமட serves as an onomatopoeic expression that mimics the sound of water being gulped down. It emphasises the manner in which she is drinking the water—quickly and with noticeable gulps. The full translation of the sentence can be interpreted as: *'She is drinking the water with a "madamada" sound.'*

8.4. Uses of -உம் suffix

The -உம் suffix has various uses in Tamil, with its most common function being a conjunction that translates to **and** in English. It is utilised to connect nouns or phrases, indicating that two or more elements or concepts are being considered collectively. Additionally, this suffix can convey different meanings in various contexts. Most common uses of -உம் outlined below.

1. **And** - Connects two nouns, implying an addition.
   அம்மா**வும்** தங்கச்சி**யும்** தேத்தணி குடிக்கினம்.
   Mother and little sister are drinking tea.

   என்ர அப்பாவும் நானும் கடைக்கு போறம்.
   My father and I are going to the shop.

2. **Also / additionally / too**
   Indicates that something is included in addition to what has already been mentioned.

   அம்மாவும் கடைக்கு வாறா.
   Amma is also coming to the shop.

   நானும் சாப்பிடுவென்.
   I'll eat, too.

113

3. Even though / although

Expresses concessions, indicating that despite a certain condition, something else still holds true.

கனக்க சாப்பிட்டும் எனக்கு பசிக்கிது.
Even though I ate a lot, I'm hungry.

அவா நித்திரை கொண்டும், களைப்பா இருக்கிறா.
Even though she slept, she is tired.

4. Even / even if / despite

When combined with the conditional suffix -ஆல், the -உம் suffix expresses various conditions or scenarios.

மழெ பெஞ்சாலும் நான் வெளீல போவென்.
Even if it rains, I will go outside.

5. Either / or Presents alternatives.

நீங்கள் தனியவும் வரலாம் என்ர அம்மாவோடெயும் வரலாம். You can come alone or come with my mother.

6. Neither / no - Indicates negation for multiple subjects.

அம்மாவும் இல்லெ நானும் இல்லெ.
Neither amma nor me.

Bibliography

ஆறுமுக நாவலர் (1993). *தமிழ் இலக்கணம் (இலக்கணச் சுருக்கம்) (Tamil Ilakkanam - Ilakkanach Churukkam)*, சென்னை: முல்லை நிலையம்.

இராமநாதன், பொன்னம்பலம் (2018). செந்தமிழ் இலக்கணம் (Centamil Ilakkanam), சென்னை: அடிஸன் அச்சுக்கூடம்.

கங்காதரம், ம. (1997). தமிழ் எழுத்துகள். நேற்று - இன்று - நாளை (Thamizh Ezhuthukal. Netru - Indru - Naalai), சென்னை: காந்தளகம்.

கழகப் புலவர் குழு (2000). கழகத் தமிழ் இலக்கணம் (Kazhakath Thamizh Ilakkanam), திருநெல்வேலி: சைவ சித்தாந்த நூற்பதிப்புக் கழகம்.

சண்முகம், செ. வை. (1980). எழுத்திலக்கணக் கோட்பாடு (Ezhuthilakkanak Kotpaadu). அண்ணாமலைநகர்: அனைத்திந்தியத் தமிழ்மொழியியல் கழகம்.

தமிழ் இணையக் கல்விக்கழகம் (2024, October 4). இடைச்சொல் இலக்கணம் (Idaichol Ilakkanam). https://www.tamilvu.org/courses/degree/a051/a0512/html/a0512315.htm

நூஃமான், எம். ஏ. (1999). *அடிப்படைத் தமிழ் இலக்கணம் (Adippadaith Thamizh Ilakkanam)*, கல்முனை: வாசகர் சங்கம்.

பவானி, மா. (2024, October 4). கிரந்தம் (Kirantham). Tamil Virtual University. https://www.tamilvu.org/tdb/titles_cont/inscription/html/treatise.htm

மாணிக்கவாசகன், ஞா. (2006). தொல்காப்பியம் - மூலமும் விளக்க உரையும் (Tholkapiyam - Mulamum Vilakka Uraiyum), சென்னை: உமா பதிப்பகம்.

Appasamy Murugaiyan. Focus Constructions in Modern Tamil. *International Journal of Dravidian Linguistics*, 2009, 38(2), pp.43-69.

Arokianathan, S. (1981). Tamil clitics. In Dravidian Linguistics Association (Ed.), Trivandrum: Dravidian Linguistics Association.

Caldwell, R. (1875). A Comparative Grammar of the Dravidian or South-Indian Family of Languages. Asian Educational Services, New Delhi, India.

Lehman, T. (1993). A grammar of Modern Tamil, Pondicherry: Pondicherry Institute of Language and Culture.

Nardog, T. (2024). Vocal Tract Images, licensed under CC BY-SA 4.0. https://commons.wikimedia.org/wiki/File:VocalTract.svg

Pappuswamy, U. (2005). Dative Subjects in Tamil: A Computational Analysis. *South Asian Language Review*, *43*(XV).

Salomon, R. (1998). *Indian epigraphy: A guide to the study of inscriptions in Sanskrit, Prakrit and other languages.* Oxford University Press.

Schiffman, H. (1999). A Reference Grammar of Spoken Tamil. Cambridge: Cambridge UniversityPress.

South Asia Language Resource Centre (2024, December 10). Adverbial Participle Form. http://learn.tamilnlp.com/grammar/tamilgrammar28.html

Steever, S. B. (2005). The Tamil Auxiliary System. New York: Routledge.